WAITING IN THE WINGS

Other books by the author

Native Country of the Heart: A Memoir

A Xicana Codex of Changing Consciousness: Writings 2000–2010

Watsonville: Some Place Not Here /
Circle in the Dirt: El Pueblo de East Palo Alto

The Hungry Woman: A Mexican Medea /
The Heart of the Earth: A Popol Vuh Story

Heroes and Saints & Other Plays

The Last Generation

Giving Up the Ghost

Loving in the War Years: Lo que nunca pasó pos sus labios

Cuentos: Stories by Latinas (coeditor)

This Bridge Called My Back: Writings by Radical Women of Color
(coeditor)

WAITING IN THE WINGS
PORTRAIT OF A QUEER MOTHERHOOD
CHERRÍE MORAGA

25th Anniversary Edition
with a new preface by the author
and an afterword by Rafael Angel Moraga

Haymarket Books
Chicago, IL

Published in 2022 by
Haymarket Books
P.O. Box 180165
Chicago, IL 60618
773-583-7884
www.haymarketbooks.org
info@haymarketbooks.org

ISBN: 978-1-64259-830-8

Distributed to the trade in the US through Consortium Book Sales
and Distribution (www.cbsd.com) and internationally through
Ingram Publisher Services International (www.ingramcontent.com).

This book was published with the generous support of Lannan Foun-
dation and Wallace Action Fund.

Special discounts are available for bulk purchases by organizations
and institutions. Please email info@haymarketbooks.org for more
information.

Cover photo from the collection of Cherríe Moraga. All rights
reserved. Cover design by Rachel Cohen.

Printed in Canada by union labor.

Library of Congress Cataloging-in-Publication data is available.

10 9 8 7 6 5 4 3 2 1

To that hole in my heart,
Rafael Angel Moraga,
thank you for staying

And in gratitude to the nurses at San Francisco Kaiser ICN, 1993

Contents

Preface

Portrait of a Writer

As a cultivated writing praxis, creative nonfiction allows for a broader panorama of experience than a genre restricted to the empirical. It is one that permits dreams to presage, and queer bodies to serve as repositories of, memory. With the best of intentions, I believe *Waiting in the Wings* does just that, perhaps even more so from the historical perspective of twenty-five years since its original publication in 1997.

Wings offers a queer view of motherhood and mothering from an era preceding national legalization of same-sex marriage and gay adoption. Discussions of nonbinary gender identification and queer sexuality, along the more generous gender continuum we know today, were not the LGBT lingua franca of the early '90s, nor was the acronym widely employed, or the "T" in the acronym. At that time, in my neighborhood in San Francisco, trans Latina public visibility was largely restricted to the drag shows at Esta Noche on Valencia & 16th.*

---

* Also, in the same neighborhood in the early nineties, CURAS and El Proyecto Contra SIDA por Vida, grew out of the AIDS pandemic, serving the Latinx queer communities, significantly transwomen.

Looking back has given me pause.

Although I am grateful for, and beholden to, the activists whose struggles secured us queers our twenty-first-century rights, I ask myself if legalization and all the language we accumulated along the road to achieving it might not have also unwittingly convinced us we were free. For many queer people, it might as well be the 1950s and 1960s of my childhood, with liberation still "waiting in the wings." For them, and for us, who imagine ourselves thoroughly "enlightened" about our queerness, I believe *Wings* may offer a different road to wholeness. It excavates buried questions, exposes contradictions hardly understood in the body. In retrospect, the writing seems marked by the yet unseen, by the failed to mention but known by heart. Inscribed by a Chicana/Xicana/Xicanx queer mother, I believe the work speaks to a bit of what remains missing in "America's" national consciousness.

Waiting in the Wings began as journal entries; a record of my forty-year-old lesbian genderqueer* self in the act of becoming pregnant and giving birth. But within months of that initial journaling, the writing became something unanticipated, something I had only witnessed in dreams, anxiously recorded on the page. It became a meditation on death and dying. I had seen death coming down the road, first in the shrinking fragility of the old ones in my familia, not yet of my mother's generation, but that of *her* mother—a ninety-six-year-old twig of tenacity splintering into the embrace de la muerte.

On my paternal side, from early childhood, I still hold the distant memory of the other grandma, the white one. After a stroke, her flaccid skin melted onto her skeletal frame as surreal to my young eyes as a Dalí painting.

---

* That is, "masculine of center." Neither was in our queer vocabulary at that time.

Fast-forward to decades later when AIDS entered our queer world, turning some of the most brown and beautiful jotos* into old men overnight. The women followed soon after. Margarita and I are dancing in an Acapulco Bar one summer, and by the next, she disappears into the obscurity of SIDA. This was the world in which I would give birth to my son, just shy of my twenty-eighth week of pregnancy, on July 3, 1993.

Suddenly the *what happened* of the journal writing was eclipsed by *What will become of us?* I very quickly learned what it meant to carry *susto* in the body; to no longer trust the universe to be on one's side. To pray for the best and ready yourself for the worst. I also learned the daily gift of survival, its necessary faith, and the willingness to accept loss.

In my 2010 *Xicana Codex of Changing Consciousness*, I called the perilous birth of my son and the slow Alzheimer's dying of my mother in 2005 "bookends." The former would prepare me for the latter. There were others in between and after: Marsha, Ingrid, Mahsa. (*Will I ever grow tired of writing their names?*) This, the litany of loss that profoundly changed my worldview. All would require of me a different kind of writer. But, without exception, confronting death in the creative locus of giving birth to Rafael Angel welded a warriorship in me to meet all the rest that followed.

The experience described in these pages matters in the repertoire of queer literatures. Because the mandate of art, and I would like to believe queer art especially, is to account for unspoken truths in which the equations do not always add up. Like so many others, my queerness has never added up exactly into neat categories of sex, gender, and sexuality; and yet it has shaped who I am every step of the way, including throughout nearly three decades of mothering.

---

* Latino queer men.

My female sex was determined at birth, and I rebelled against its socialization to the degree possible as an utterly tomboy child, followed by a suffering, closeted, trans-terrified and woman-lusting adolescent, to eventually emerge into a butch-identified adult lesbian. This is old and common language, but true to my experience, coming of age in the late 1960s.

What I hadn't realized was the degree to which my self-perception as a *butch* lesbian would be so profoundly impacted by the somatic act of motherhood: the hormonal changes, the breastfeeding, the sudden rush of adrenaline with every new threat to my son's life. I have never been able to forget—nor would I want to forget—what was learned there.

Birthing confirmed for me on an utterly corporeal level that female sex in no way requires one to "present" as a woman in the socialized sense of the word. It viscerally reminded me that "female" simply describes biology and that I had a right to that biology in my own gendered version of it, should I so choose. For me, my anatomical sex wasn't wrong. The world is wrong about any gendered imposition on that sex, something intersex people have long publicly asserted.

It is also a feminist and queer right to insist that womanhood in whatever way one understands it (including as trans women) matters politically in a misogynist world. It remains an oppressed class among humans as we walk in our gendered and (for women of color) racially marked bodies every day of our lives. Oh, I know it is all more complicated than this.* But I got a taste of what it is like to experience the female animal I am, and it was something I took hold of toward the whole of me. Perhaps this is what trans folk have been trying to teach

---

* Discussions on the relationship between biological sex and gender continue to evolve, as does my understanding.

us all along—their rightful entitlement, with the aid of hormones (and surgery for some), to get the biological sex "right" in order to experience that same wholeness of being.[*]

◆ ◆ ◆

In the larger landscape of this story, it is 1993, and Rafaelito is already a presence in my womb. Together, we attend our first Medicine Ceremony. The Roadman, William Baker, sits behind the sacred fire, officiating. It is a "manly" affair, and I have recently learned of my baby's male sex. I speak to my son, a knowing spirit growing inside me. We begin a lifelong dialogue—mother to son.

Last summer, twenty-eight years later, Rafa would return, now a grown man, to that same Roadman's ceremonial fireplace, this time guided by the hand of a faithful stepbrother. Days later, on Roadman Baker's way home from that ceremony, he, and his twelve-year-old grandson would be killed in a car crash.

In the twenty-five years since the publication of *Waiting in the Wings*, my son's life and my own continue to weave together threads of connections—of beginnings and endings—which direct us to the next step in our lives.

What does this tragic loss mean? We ask.

Where do we go from here, this time?

Two and half decades later, the subtitle of this work resonates for me more deeply than ever. It is, indeed, a very "queer" tale; but today, knowing my son as a young man, I understand more fully that this work is less a story about him and much more about what I learned mothering his endangered birth and insistence on life. He has his own

---

[*] Today trans men can and do become pregnant and give birth consistent with their own sense of well-being.

story to tell and live—with a view toward a future I will not witness, as he did not bear witness to my past.*

Such is life and death and life again.

June 2022
Santa Bárbara, California
Anisq'oyo

---

* See the afterword.

Reading *Wings*

2022

Much of the writing here was first composed as journal entries, indi-cated by italics. I returned to those passages to fill in the details of events which, especially in chapters I and II, found me too immersed and utterly wordless in the living of them to describe. Chapter III is similarly drawn with italicized journal entries that were later aug-mented for clarity and context.

Throughout most of the text (with a few exceptions), I do not distinguish my occasional use of Spanish from English to allow for the natural Spanglish of this Chicana voice. My closest friends are sometimes referred to as "comadres" or "compadre," a Mexican term denoting an intimacy similar to that of a family member, not to be confused with "co-mothers" or "co-fathers" in English.

It is also important to note that I intentionally maintain the 1996 usage of gender pronouns and the gender binary spellings of words in Spanish, e.g., Chicana/Chicano, for this feels truer to the portrait of the times in which the original work was written. I have also added foot-notes to contextualize certain moments historically and/or politically.

Finally, although the work is chronologically driven, I have at times reconfigured the order of events in favor of the requirements of dramatic storytelling.

In retrospect, I see this book as a kind of poet's memoir, for even giving birth does not satisfy the artist's desire to create.

We do not know where death awaits us:

so let us wait for it everywhere.

To practice death is to practice freedom.

A man who has learned how to die

has unlearned how to be a slave.

—Michel de Montaigne

Prologue

The Long Hard Path

1996

It's like making familia from scratch—
each time all over again.
With strangers, if I must.
If I must, I will.

—Moraga, *Giving Up the Ghost*

L **esbians don't make babies with our lovers.**
We make babies with strangers in one-night stands or on
the doctor's insemination table, with friends in a friendly fuck or an
indifferent mason jar, with enemies who at the time were husbands or
boyfriends, or with ex-husbands whom our children call "papi" and
whom we may still consider family. We cannot make babies with one
another. Our blood doesn't mix into the creation of a third entity with
an equal split of DNA. Sure, we can co-adopt, we can coparent, we can
be comadres, but blood mami and papi we ain't.*

---

* In 1996, transgender pregnancies were scarcely publicly discussed and little

I know the stories that we only admit to one another in private, our children's hunger for "normalcy," no matter how much they love us. Maria, a brilliant butch woman, told me years ago about a boy she had raised with his mother for many years. One night her heart broke when, tucking in the bespectacled boy of ten, he wrapped his arms around her neck and called her "daddy" with everything he had in him. When I finally met the boy, I saw that he shared Maria's poor eyesight, wit, and brainy humor. Most of all, he learned how to be a boy from Maria. He learned masculinity from Maria and she was a wonderful male role model: the best of fathers with a woman's compassion.[*]

I have been the lesbian lover of a mother. I know what it is to live in that uncertain role as the "nonbiological parent"—such a cold Anglo-American term.[†] But at least in the beginning, and perhaps on a deeper level, I asked the same of my partner, Ellen. I asked her not to be a mother, but only a lover of my child, a lover to me. Probably hers is the most noble, the bravest, of gestures—to walk this path without inscribed guarantees.

In the beginning, I didn't know how much mother Ellen would be to our child. Neither did she. I didn't know how much I wanted to share motherhood. I didn't know how soft and hard that letting go would be: to entrust another human being with the raising of your child. I have, at times, rigorously protected my single-motherhood for

---

was known about the medical options in this regard.

[*] The portrait I paint here depicts an era when same-sex second-parent adoptions were not as ubiquitous as they are today, even in my home state of California.

[†] I refer here to the relationship between the blood mother, her child, and her partner. When a lesbian adopts or co-adopts a child with her partner, parental rights in relation to the child are interpreted, and may be experienced, quite differently.

fear of losing my son to *anyone*. Still, I suspect that I would not have embarked on this journey alone. I chose motherhood because I knew Ellen was that quality of person who would never just up and leave.

"I'm going to do this," I told her. "Will you go there with me?" Had Ellen answered no, quite possibly I would have gone no further.

I imagine most people would think it radical to take it upon one's lesbian self to make such a proposal first to her partner, and then to a gay man, several years younger. *I'm going to do this. Will you help me?* Without question in another era, in another geographical region outside of San Francisco, another cultural point of reference, my having a baby as an avowed lesbian would have been a radical phenomenon indeed. And in most circles, I imagine it still is. But not in my own circle, not in the circle where I have constructed familia, not with a woman partner as firm as the steady changing earth, not among the women I call comadres, the donor I now call compadre, nor among my blood familia. Having Rafael Angel was the most natural evolution of two lives—his and my own—the most logical next step on a road whose mysterious twists and turns make me marvel daily.

I tell friends that I almost missed Rafaelito. That he had been there, waiting in the wings, and I could hear his voice in the most remote corners of my dreams and in the raising of other women's children. That is how I account for his precipitous birth at only twenty-eight weeks of gestation. He was a spirit who, for some time, was wanting to get here, through me. And when I finally opened my heart and listened, he took hold of me right away. I was pregnant with the first home insemination. Six months later he was born, weighing only two pounds, six ounces.

Upon the news of my pregnancy, Myrtha, one of my most beloved friends, una poeta feminista puertorriqueña, said to me, "Te admiro, you're doing it your own way." Now sixty, Myrtha had raised three sons almost single-handedly. What was there to admire in me? But I understood what she meant. I had come to my motherhood along the long hard path. Nothing has been a given for me, not even my womanhood.

Growing up, the *we* of my life was always defined by blood relations.

We meant familia.

We were my mother's children, my abuela's grandchildren, my tíos' nieces and nephews. I was blessed to be born into a huge extended Mexican family. A familia in which aunts and uncles acted as surrogate parents, and cousins were counted among siblings, and where my grandmother, Dolores, who lived to the age of ninety-six, presided matriarchal over the lives of some one-hundred-plus relatives. Today, the living Moraga clan spans five generations and a full century of US-born mestizos, residing in what was once the Mexican territory of Alta California and, before that and always, *Native Country.*

My parents, now in their seventies and eighties, live in the same house that I have known since the age of nine. My sense of home was formed both inside the walls of that 1920s stucco two-and-a-half-bedroom suburban Los Angeles structure as much as it has been shaped outside of it. When I return to visit, I sleep in the same room (now "the TV room") where my sister and I, as teenagers in the 1960s, shared apocalyptic nightmares and tormented dreams of sexual awakening (although I knew even then that the shape of her dreams was very different from my own).

To this day, most of my cousins still hold onto that shared *we* understanding of familia. Not I. In 1975, at the age of twenty-two, I came out as a lesbian and named as female the figures in those nocturnal adolescent desirous dreamscapes. Once out, although I did not keep my sexuality secret from the closest members of my family, I knew it could never be fully expressed there. So the search for a *we* that could embrace all the parts of myself took me far beyond the confines of heterosexual family ties. I soon found myself spinning outside the orbit of that familial embrace, separated by thousands of miles of geography and experience. Still, the need for familia, the knowledge of familia, the capacity to create familia remained and has always informed my relationships and my work as an artist, cultural activist, and teacher.

I've always experienced my lesbianism as culturally distinct from most white gays and lesbians. For that reason, I have never been a strong proponent of gay marriage (although I've officiated a few weddings). Perhaps this reflects my feminist of color resistance to any imposition of social convention prescribed by privileged sectors of liberation movements. No, I've always longed for something else in my relationships—something woman-centered, something extended and multigenerational, something less privatized. In short, something Mexican and familial but without all the patriarchal constraints.

Rosie hunches over the pages of her notebook, blocking her tight-fisted scrawl with the draping sleeve of her flannel shirt. She is my student. At fifteen, Rosie has more piercings etched into her flesh than her number of years on the planet. She puts down her pen and looks up at me with wide eyes. "Am I doomed?" she asks with those eyes. I know her family story—the brutal fact of abuse, the white rapist father, the silent Latina mother. So she cuts at her body and drives ink and all manner of rings into her skin. She sticks liquid needles into her veins and wonders if she'll survive the season. The season of being young and queer and on the street because home is a more dangerous place to be. She is my daughter.*

---

* For five years, in the early 1990s, I directed a writing-for-performance queer

I want something more than 12-step for Rosie and her Latina lesbian kind. She deserves more than Christianity or goddess worship, more than politically correct lines that take away our edges, our outrage, nuestra pasión. She deserves familia resurrected and repaired, by *us*.

My search for this familia has been played out (at times with misguided tenacity) with every lover I have had, regardless of age or race or cultural background. With each one, I thought myself committed for the duration, for, surely, we were at war trying to make a place for lesbian love in a woman-hating world. And as I tried to "save" each one of my lovers, and all her children (those incarnate and those invisible), the invisible wreaked havoc on our loving: the rapes, the incest, the battering, the betrayals, the alcoholism, the orphanhood. Even as we repeat the scenarios, we try to repair, for better or worse, the familial lessons we learned about loving.

There was a time for me when my sense of family, and by extension community, was mostly women, then mostly lesbian, then mostly women of color, then mostly Raza, then mostly Latina lesbian. (Not always in that order.) But these categories of identity could never fully encompass the people in whom I placed my trust. In each of those worlds I found abrazo y rechazo and I soon learned to make home within that less-defined realm of shared values and the daily praxis that comes with it.

As a child and a tomboy, I had never fantasized about having kids. No more than most little boys do, dreaming about a brood of five sons— enough to make up a basketball team. When I came out as a lesbian at the age of twenty-two, I had simply assumed that since I would never

---

youth theater troupe in San Francisco called the DramaDIVAS. "Rosie" was one of its most significant members.

be married to a man, I would never have children. This may sound strange, given that as far as I knew I was technically *capable* of getting pregnant. But buried deep inside me, regardless of the empirical evidence to the contrary, I had maintained the rigid conviction that lesbians (that is, those of us on the more masculine side of the spectrum) weren't really women. We were women-lovers, a kind of "third sex," and most definitely not men. Having babies was something "real" women did—not butches, not girls who knew they were queer since grade school. We were the *defenders* of women and children, children we could never fully call our own.

"**A**ll you really got are your children."
        In my mid-thirties, I was involved with a wonderful artist and her young child, whom I will call Joel. In the three years of my relationship with his mother, I had grown to think of Joel—whether sanctioned or not—as my own. Then one day, I lost them both without warning and with great wrenching. Not so much from the woman, as from the child. This was the baby I had watched become a boy, whom I had walked to kindergarten, taught how to ride a two-wheeler and build sandcastles on the beach. We had hiked in the foothills together, I pointing out leaf and flor. I had explained the meaning of morning frost to him, the metamorphosis of polliwogs to frogs, of caterpillar to marvelous mariposa. And I had also made his morning breakfast, bathed him in the evening, picked him up from day care, and given him medicine in the middle of the night. I didn't do these things equally to his mother, but I was a partner to her and a parent to him to the degree that I was allowed. Simply, I knew Joel with a kind of heart's knowledge that I have never been able to completely erase.

I remember once, just before the official breakup, Joel and I had been separated from his mother and each other for many weeks. He had been staying with his father, and after much urging from me, the man let me have Joel overnight. The first thing I did was give Joel a much-needed bath. Pulling him out of the tub, I wrapped him in a huge cotton towel and took to grooming him, tenderly cleaning his ears with a Q-tip, clipping his finger- and toenails, rubbing his smooth cafecito skin with sweet oil. Suddenly, he looked up at me and blurted out, "You're my mom." We both were missing her badly. And at that moment I could already taste their forever-absence in my life.

The one time I was allowed to see Joel after a six-month separation, he became very angry in our last hour together and refused to hold my hand. At the time, I didn't understand. We had gone on an overnight camping trip and had built a toy-sized grave for his abuelo, who had recently passed. We constructed the cross out of tiny twigs. I had felt so close to Joel then, making up our own ceremony for a man who had eaten at my table and yet whose death I learned of thirdhand. Joel's sudden anger as we parted hurt me, but later I realized maybe it was also too painful for him, these long absences and strained reunions.

Driving the six-hour trip back to San Francisco alone, I barely missed what could have been a fatal car accident. I cursed my car and raged against my predicament, my lack of bona fide motherhood *or* fatherhood, and the absolute impotence of being the lesbian lover of a mother.

Men (and women) come and go, I could hear my mother's refrain.
All you really got are your children.
But Mamá, I lost the child, too.

The dreams where Joel appears, always in crisis, have gradually dissipated with the birth of my son. Still, I think of Joel often. Kindly, sadly.

I remember one incident when I was putting Rafaelito back into his car seat after shopping, and I called him "Joel." The word just slipped out into the air, never to be retrieved. I felt guilty, I wasn't sure why, and I assured my son, *Tú eres el único, hijo,* the way we must reassure our lovers when by accident we call them by a past lover's name. When this happens between lovers, we are mortified. *What does it mean?* We fear that the other beloved was the greater love. And sometimes she was. But sometimes she was merely a profound touching, an awakening that will always be remembered by that original name, even when the same place is touched by another. That is who Joel is to me, my first (almost) son. And the mother he called forth in me made my hunger for Rafael Angel all the more urgent: a child that would never be taken from me, a child to raise from scratch.

One thing Joel's presence in my life taught me was that, without realizing it, I had grown up to be woman enough, on my own terms, to mother a child. The child grew inside me, the loss of the child, the discovery of mother, the recognition that I had nursed dozens of hungry women throughout my life as I had my own mother, from the time I could remember, and in that resided my lesbian conviction, my lesbian loving. I am a daughter and have always loved those daughters in all our beauty and brokenness. *But what of the children?*

Not until 1992, a handful of years after the loss of Joel, could I answer that question unequivocally and affirmatively: I wanted a child.

I was forty years old.

San Francisco
Ramaytush Ohlone land

I

CITY OF THE ANGELS

1993

An angel came to me last night
sat patient in the fog
of my night sweats . . .

His tears washed away
my lesions
said he wanted me
to . . . heal the earth . . .

Leave my mark
with my halting steps . . .

He wanted me
to fly.

—Tede Matthews, "Angel Wings"

6 de enero / San Francisco

The feast of the epiphany—good day to start a life.
When Ellen and Ricardo sat around me on my bed after the insemination, a comforter covering me, my legs propped up in the air with pillows, I felt "made love to." That's the expression that came to mind, and that was the feeling exactly. The way I always imagined becoming pregnant would feel like, in the best of scenarios. But the insemination had nothing to do with sex or orgasm or excitement, except our three-way titillated embarrassment over the procedure.

Ricardo sat in the bathroom, trying to think about anything sexier than the mouth of a mason jar, while Ellen and I waited nervously in the bedroom together, Ellen practicing pumping water in and out of the syringe. Still, for all its awkwardness, I can say that the experience was probably the best loving I'd ever known. I am still awed by the fact that these two people loved me enough to go through whatever embarrassment to help me conceive.

"That's all there was to it?" Ellen's mom would ask us months later.

"Yes."

"But it's so simple."

"Yeah," I answer. "One way or another that sperm has just gotta get inside you."

Very simple . . . and unromantic. Yet I did feel made love to. And whether pregnant or not, I knew I would never forget what that softness felt like, my legs up and open to receive whatever destiny had decided for me.

3

I close my eyes and dream Ricardo as a sweet twin lover. I put my mouth and nose into the hollow of Ellen's neck, breathe her in and I am sustained. Momentarily, there is tranquilidad.

28 enero / Los Angeles

Today I feel my hormones acting up, blowing me up, sitting heavy on my chest. I wonder if this is all just a bad case of PMS. I wonder if I am pregnant. I feel my body a stranger. I am without desire. What happened to desire? Or is it that my desire is so great and lies muted somewhere inside me.

I wish I knew how to pray. I clasp together my hands before my altar, light a vela, study la Virgen's impassive expression, wave the scent and heat of copal over all my openings and long for una respuesta—a word, an image, a vision. Does the journeying I must make right now involve miles of physical territory, or is it an interior map I need to explore through reading, reflection, conversation? I proceed with the plan of having a baby because I have only myself, the kindness of friends, the cosmos to trust. I experience pain often in my womb and vagina. I don't understand the signs. I ignore them, yet I know that having this baby requires listening to my body, requires diet, exercise, counsel, prayer, apoyo, hogar, fuerza, y paciencia.

I am on the verge of tears in this writing. I keep getting flashbacks, mental glimpses of my parents waiting for me at the Hollywood/Burbank airport. With each visit, they seem a bit smaller physically, a bit older, slightly more vulnerable. Standing at the gate, they greet me with expectant, anxious eyes, my dad always noticing me a few seconds after my mom. I am filled with emotion. This family means so much to me, this family slipping away. I grow to comprehend, somewhere in my heart, how tran-

sitory this physical life is. I miss LA in certain way. I miss how I am essentially LA born and bred, but my spirit resides elsewhere.

29 enero

Returning from the play reading in Los Angeles, I ignore what is most evident—my desire for this child. I give it half-hearted attention, not being able to fully believe it could happen to me. In the deepest places I am as afraid of the commitment as I am of the disappointment. I am afraid to want this baby and be unable to have it. My sister and Ellen both try to convince me to take a home pregnancy test, but I am superstitious. I think if I want it too bad, it won't happen.

Finally, coming back from LA, I promise Ellen that if she buys the test, I'll take it. She does. In seconds after I put the required few drops of urine onto the test paper, two pink lines appear indicating I'm pregnant. There is no ambivalence in those lines; they are a dark, solid, unwavering pink, and there are clearly two of them. Ellen and I look at each other, dumbfounded. I still can't believe it. How could two tiny lines, such insignificant markings, pronounce something as irrevocable as a human life? Ellen can't believe my resistance. She volunteers to take the test. If hers turns up with only one line, then will I be convinced? Yes, I promise. Sure enough, one line and a faint one at that. We stare at each other in the bathroom, looking back and forth at her test and mine . . . her test and mine. Ellen's eyes are dancing with excitement, but I can't fully take it in and make a silent agreement not to count on any babies until I get a blood test from the doctor. It isn't denial, exactly, more like, *This is too good to be true.*

30 enero

*It is nearly February, and I realize that in weeks I am to take off
to Guatemala for the Popol Vuh project.* *But I have made no
plans, and I grow tired at the thought of it. I don't know why,
but I think of staying home. Reading all I can on the Popol Vuh,
beginning to work on* The Hungry Woman,† *slowing down. I
think of visiting la partera, Angelina, seeking her consejo about
this maybe-baby, improving my diet, my exercise regimen. For
some reason, without fully wanting to admit it, I just want to take
care of myself.*

3 febrero

Just got a call from the doctor. Bona fide pregnant. First try.

I haven't written of my days with the reproductive sciences, the fertility experts, the sonograms of my fetus-sized fibroids—all benign and
thoroughly unproductive. I had all the tests months ago, in advance, to
make sure everything was in working order "down there"—the tubes
clear, the hormones balanced—in short, a healthy habitat. The fertility
specialist had given me the odds: bad even for forty-year-old heterosex-
uals who are "doing it all the time," he said. Still, I'd give it a shot. How?
He wanted to know but didn't ask. Weeks later, when I came in with the
news of my pregnancy, whispering to the nurses, "It was homemade,"
they all cracked up, teasing the Doc. So much for science. He took it in
good stride, even came to see my baby, months later in the Intesive Care
Nursery (ICN), telling me he had never seen me look so happy.

---

* During the time of this writing, I was working on *Heart of the Earth*, a play adap-
tation of the *Popol Vuh*, the Quiché Maya creation myth and twin heroes' story.

† Subtitled *A Mexican Medea*, it is a play based on the Greek tragedy and the
Mexican myth of La Llorona (The Weeping Woman).

15 febrero

I dream two images of my baby. One where he is born already a grown boy. So beautiful, so sensuous. I touch him all over. I can't believe he is mine, although I am disappointed that he was born a boy. I touch his penis inside his pants. I know I have gone too far, but I am delighting so much in his beauty.

Then my baby is born again. This time a tiny, beautiful, dark haired Mexican girl. I am in heaven. I remember looking at the baby girl's genitalia, thinking at first the swollen round vagina was a soft scrotum, then realizing, no, it is a vagina. The joy is endless, although throughout both parts of the dream I wonder how it is my baby was born so fast when she was just nothing more than a seed inside of me. She is transparent. Her skin a see-through casing, holding in muscle and bone. I know in the dream that the skin will take on the appearance of flesh later. Of this, I am convinced.

19 febrero

This baby settles into me. If I were to write about being a writer, I would say it has something to do with the contemplative life, the life of standing at the end of a pier, the sun an hour into the horizon of black bay waters. The skyscraper reflections make me believe that at forty my life is barely beginning. I know it is this life I carry within me that causes me to imagine a future, a future I could never dream in any lover, only in blood familia, only in my sister with whom I shared a bedroom and a dream-life for twenty years. As girls we believed we would never be parted.

I stare into the black sea and know my eyes mirror that same endless dark depth. I float out under the Golden Gate Bridge and into the Pacific, knowing with complete clarity that my life will take me (us) to many lands, to many languages. How is it that travel seems more possible now, thinking of this life . . . this barely formed being? I walk back to my car at a brisk pace. Driving home, the radio announces the Senate passage of a bill outlawing the entrance of HIV-infected immigrants. One reporter speaks of 270 Haitians imprisoned in camps; "a living hell," he calls it. And a prayer rises up to my lips. "We all, each one of us, deserve a future."

I return home to cook catfish. Full of gratitude for such abundance, the barriers between Ellen and me dissolve. And I think, Perhaps we may never be parted.

28 febrero

It is barely past midnight when I awaken, trembling from the nightmare. I only remember Ellen's face, like my sister's, but with a bottomless rage. My entire body fills with the fire of fear first, then despair. I do everything in my power to calm her down. It is too late; all I can do is escape the dream. I will myself awake. My body bounds with adrenaline. I feel the new life inside me stir. And I think of how this small smudge of life knows me like no other; how once I knew my mother in the same way and was born with the knowledge of her torment. This is not the legacy I wish to pass on to my baby.

More dreams. I am bleeding, not heavily, but not exactly spotting either. I try to call the nurse, to no avail. It is late when I arrive at the hospital. The day is done. She is irritated. "Are you really bleeding or just spotting?" she asks. I feel guilty, embarrassed that I am not sure, that I may be overly worried.

1 marzo

My skin has broken out in a desperate rash. This morning I awaken to a narrow band of pain just below my ribcage. I feel my *uterus expanding. I know the baby is larger now. Its presence is irrevocable, and the gravity of this change hits a deeper level. I go back to bed hoping the pain will subside. It does. I awaken to the sound of the boiling kettle. Ellen is up.*

I think of how my baby will be born in the year of Myrtha's mother's death. I never got to meet her, never got to Puerto Rico as I had promised. Instead, the woman came to me in a dream last night and spoke the name of Refugio. Is this the name of my daughter? But, in my family history, Refugio was a distant bisabuela with hazel eyes and Indian trenzas. I never met her, either, born and buried in the Sonoran Desert a century preceding me. Possibly she spoke to me of "refugio," that she was seeking some, or that I needed to take refuge; find sanctuary someplace other than where I had been looking. Or maybe she wanted me to shelter her youngest and aging daughter, my Myrtha. And the cycle continues.

2 marzo

The results of the CVS test* are in. Ellen and I are on extension phones as we hear the genetic specialist tell us the baby is a boy. "That's good news, isn't it?'" she asks. I smile weakly. "Yes, of course. Yes, thank you." We hang up. Speechless.

The day before, the specialist left word on the answering machine that the test had shown the baby to be perfectly normal genetically. I didn't realize how worried I had been until I replayed the recording and burst into tears. I didn't know I had been holding my breath for those first twelve weeks, fearing to tell anyone I was pregnant (outside my closest circle of comadres) in the event the baby would not be as

---

* A prenatal test, given the late age of my pregnancy.

healthy as one hopes. After all, I was forty years old and pregnant for the first time. So the question of the baby's sex came later, as an afterthought, when one has the luxury to ruminate over such details.

I confess the news of a baby boy came as a shock to both of us. Naïve as it may seem, we believed we were getting a girl, if for no other reason than we had done the insemination early in my cycle (too early, really) for me to get pregnant. The reasoning was that I was rushing off for a week in New York and by its end I would be ovulating. Rather than waiting another full month, Ellen, Ricardo, and I decided to get the "virgin voyage," so to speak, over with on the long chance that insemination might take.

When I learned I was pregnant, I figured all the Y chromosomes had long ago taken their leave since they are fast swimmers of short duration. I figured wrong. In the end, I realized science had nothing to do with it. This baby was a soul wanting to get here as a male. Punto final. Later Ellen asks, "What will you name him?" "Rafael," I answer, no doubt in my mind. I have always loved the name.

Ellen suggests we go to the local bookstore to look up the name to see what message it might bring. In The Book of Saints, *I find "Rafael" listed among the other archangels. "The healing power of God," it states. "Patron of musicians and travelers." "Perfect," I say aloud. And I am more reconciled as I see at the bottom of the listing that Rafael Angel's feast day falls on my expected delivery date. September 29.*

Okay, I say to myself, I get it. Es el destino. Upon hearing the news of my baby boy, Myrtha tells me, "He will have a feminine soul."*

---

* In re-reading this journal entry twenty-five years later, I was struck by

18 marzo

Ellen calls from work and tells me Tede is sick with AIDS.* It is news I have been resisting for three days. A rumor, I told myself. But today it is confirmed, and I think only of the other news, of the boy I am to birth. There is meaning in the fact that my fetus has formed itself into a male, a meaning I must excavate from the most buried places in myself, as well as from this city, this era of dying into which my baby will be born. I understood the female, the daughter. The son holds a message I will learn to decipher with my heart.

I don't understand dying. I don't understand Tede's dying. My first thought, so selfish, I can't bear to endure another AIDS death. My brief acquaintance with it with Rodrigo left me mute, horrified. It is not the death that frightens so; it is the slow, humiliating dissolution of the body.†

I fear the face of death. I am ashamed of my fear.

The sun passes through my bedroom window, and I find hope in its afternoon warmth. I pray my baby feels it too upon his face and frail chest of pale skin within me. All day today I have been unable to write. The news of conceiving a son has shaken me

---

how fixed my notion of gender may sound in relation to the sex of the fetus; however, what prompted my initial disappointment at the news of my baby's sex had less to do with his biology and more with my own worry over what I had suffered as a queer female under patriarchy by the hands of *men*. I honestly never presumed the sex of the fetus would determine their presentation of gender. I had known too many queers along a full spectrum of gender expression in my own life to think otherwise.

* Tede Matthews was a San Francisco–based Nicaraguan solidarity worker, queer poet, and community organizer.

† Rodrigo Reyes was a Chicano joto poet and teatrista, founder of CURAS, the first SIDA/AIDS organization in San Francisco directed specifically for Latinx queer and trans folk.

profoundly. I toss the coins. The I-Ching oracles: "God has man-
ifested himself." The destiny that is joining this boy-child and me
together is out of my hands, and I open my heart to receive him.
I name him Rafael Angel. Por vida.

19 marzo

Last night, in sweating sleeplessness, I feared my baby was leav-
ing me. I feared the fevers from this flu were burning him out.
I feared there was no place for my reckoning with his maleness.
I spoke with him all night last night. I spoke to him for under-
standing amid aching joints and a low-grade fever and a steady
dampness between my thighs. I tossed and turned with images of
Medea. I still know that this is the play I must write, although
I fear it. How is it I can be pregnant and write the story of kill-
ing a child? La Llorona haunts. I must believe that my son can
forgive his mother's relentless need to describe the source of our
female deformation. It is not mere feminist rhetoric that makes a
woman stop dumbfounded in the face of a life of raising a son. It
is the living woman-wound that we spend our lives trying to heal.

This sickness es una limpieza, I tell myself. These sweats, my
own curative waters.

"I wanted a female to love," I tell Ricardo.

He answers wisely, "You've done that your entire life as a
lesbian."

Yes.

I awaken rested, cooled. It is an overcast morning, and I hear
the little neighbor girl, Morgan, descend the steps from upstairs,
chatting endlessly to her mother as she does every morning on
her way to school. This morning I hear her voice as a small boy's
voice, and it is equally tender.

22 marzo

Last night, a miserable night without sleep, unable to breathe. Spring has arrived, along with my allergies. My body is thick with fatigue. Ellen and our neighbor Ski dig up the garden, stir up new life after months of rain. I wait for this wave of illness to pass so I can return to work, so I can give my attention to the growing child within me.

At times I fear he has fallen asleep for good. I worry my own fears will turn him bitter against me. I do not feel Rafael Angel as some formless entity that I will shape with my own hands and love. He enters this planet, a soul intact. Who is this being? Some days I imagine him a bitter old man, un juez, severe and authoritative. I imagine him judging my harshness, my moods, my mean ways. At other times, I feel him a young sage-spirit, as delicate as his angelic name.

1 abril / Nueva York

I've returned to New York. Last time I was here, I was, without knowing, newly pregnant. This morning I am very pregnant . . . and alone in this Lower East Side flat. I put my fingers to a vague and lingering nostalgia for a life ten years ago (my thirty-something New York days, New York lovers) and remember. But I discover no woman of the past there, but instead the eruption of who I am today.

How do I describe that at the moment of orgasm, I feel the infant inside me curl up into a hard fist, no violence, but a hard ball of intensity swelling in my womb? And I cry for this life, this miracle, this sexuality that is happening to me unlike any I have experienced. The slightest contact evokes a response. Touching myself, remembering touching, her touching me.

*My body is not in this room. It is in a cave somewhere,
somewhere dark, somewhere fecund. Soy mujer de barro. Dirt
in the creases of my flesh, between my toes, beneath my tongue.
The animal kicks inside me, and that's all the sign of life I need.
I am female essence relieved of all burden. There is nothing else
required of me but to dwell here, pregnant.*

   I make love to it, the life.

5 abril

She knew that beauty and bearing witness
to the harsh materials of human struggle
need never contradict each other!

   —Adrienne Rich at Audre Lorde's memorial

*I didn't attend Audre's memorial. I was not among the hundreds
who came from all parts of the country to the Cathedral of St.
John the Divine to give tribute to this woman of genius, heart,
and courage. But I find myself there, there amid that "sacred
geometry," months later on this bitterly cold Saturday afternoon.
Sitting in a hard-backed chair on the stone floor of the largest
Gothic cathedral in the world, I pay my own small tribute to
Audre Lorde.*

   *In one of the wings of the cathedral, I find an alcove with
a small altar and kneeler dedicated to those who have died of
AIDS. Passing it, I see a dozen or so candles flicker on an otherwise bare prayer space. I go back to the entrance of the church
where I buy a seven-day votive and return to the alcove. I pray
for Tede, maricón, marxista, now sick with SIDA. I pray for my
own personal list of HIV-positive sisters and brothers: Margarita, Imani, Ronnie, José. And I pray for June and Pat and*

Merle—and, of course, for Audre—sister-poets gone or surviving with cancer.

8 abril / Back in San Francisco

I don't know what makes me cry, except the weight of all this change. I dream that my baby turns out whiter than I expected, but beautiful still, and talking too soon. I never got to hear his first word. Was it mami, papi, flor? This baby is already walking and talking full sentences, and I lament that I have missed something in his growing.

Awakening from the dream, I go to the washroom, begin to put the laundry into sorted piles when I discover that there is no detergent, and Ellen is to blame. No one is to blame, but I must blame someone, for some one thing not going as planned. We fight. Ridiculous. She leaves for work, and I barely let pass the sound of her tires on the gravel driveway before I am buried, face into the pillow, and weeping. My womb pressed up against the stiff mattress, I feel a slight fluttering, and I know the tears are only about this, this overwhelming pending change in our lives. I would never want to go back now, childless. But I wonder about our future. I make room for the baby and am overwhelmed by every box of baby hand-me-downs consuming the space necessary for his arrival. There is no detergent when I need to wash the clothes.

I cry.

---

* Some of the people mentioned here include: poet Ronnie Burk, theater director José Saucedo, and feminist writer-activists June Jordan, Pat Parker, and Merle Woo.

9 abril

A small cup-sized baby has erupted from my womb in my dream. It has dark hair and what seems like painted black lines for emerging features. The tiny sack of baby hangs by a cord between my legs. I keep trying to push it back inside, knowing it is not yet ready to emerge

I dream, again.

Someone old has passed on. It is not a tragic death because the age is ripe for dying. Upon hearing the news, I receive long green-stemmed flowers of some kind. They will soon blossom yellow and creative. I know it is my baby.

Upon wakening I go to the bathroom and find myself spotting more heavily than I have since the beginning of my pregnancy. It is a thick earth-brown color. I panic, then try to calm myself. I lie here in bed and ask my baby to give me a sign of life, a fluttering so I know all is well.

10 abril

I am the moon's keeper. Vigilant at 4:00 a.m., the moon rises. I dawn nocturnal. She appears in trinity, each reflection a bit more ephemeral. I rise, search out her light in peopleless bedrooms, through half-open shades. The garden is afternoon-illuminated, and the vegetables, too, grow like babies. In the distance there is el llanto of a backyard cat in heat; it's an infant's cry. Then, a city rooster's complaint.

The same sounds already dawning in San Cristóbal. I remember walking at 5:00 a.m. to its small bus station. I am not now as I once was, that woman orphaned by her lover, walking the cobblestones in the predawn silence. I am she who rises en busca de la luna, seeking mother/daughter in the moon, seeking light.

11 abril

There are days when I am afraid of life hurting us, the homophobia, the racism. When I hear of my brother (today is his birthday) asking my sister, "Was it artificial insemination or did she just get together with some guy?" the harshness in his tone chills me. Is it anger? Fear? What he wants to know is: Who is the father? Where is the man in the picture? The chasm I would have to traverse to have my brother understand who I am in this is too daunting. How can I explain what brought me to the decision to find a man, a decent young man, already a part of my queer familia and not ask him to father, but to simply help me get pregnant and be a friend to my child if he could?

"I would never speak badly of you to my child," I told Ricardo. "What you're giving us is all I want from you. It's enough."

12 abril

I can't get to the heart of my feeling here. I watch my body change daily and know I am not fully residing in it. These miserable allergies are dragging me down into a fog of anxiety, degression. The days are gorgeous, but I cannot fully appreciate them, the winds stirring up the pollen, the seeds of life. Pregnancy happening everywhere and ironically my body is reacting against it. I cling to Ellen in a way I had never imagined.

13 abril

It is impossible to concentrate on anything but this sudden exposure. I announce my pregnancy to my Indígena as Scribe writing class, and immediately I am surrounded by shock and excite-*

---

* From 1991 through 1995, I taught a weekly creative writing class entitled "Indígena as Scribe" for Chicanas, Latinas, and Native women who were

*ment and consejo: "You must get your water filtered." "You have
to be smudged in the delivery room. It freaks the hospital staff out
cuz the smoke alarms can go off." "Call my mother, la partera,
she'll deliver your baby." All good women, concerned women, all
thoroughly "Indígena" in their response to me.*

*I wonder why it is during these times that I am drawn to
myth over and over again; possibly it is this research on* Heart
of the Earth. *In the class I write, "On the first day of mourning, men arrived from the East in canoes with houses built upon
them. They came in search of the 'sun's excrement.'"*

*Somehow my giving birth involves me in this trajectory, this
continuing history of conquistadores and culture clashes, of resis-
tencia and regeneration.*

Nation. Nationality. I am to be the mother of a Mexican baby. I
selected a young man for his brains and dark beauty. And the race
continues. But mostly I chose Ricardo because I knew he loved
me without wanting me. A gay man. A queer contract. And I gotta
gringa-girl lover with a Spanish that don't make a fool outta her. This
is my home. For now. I don't know what the future will bring. We try
to get what we can on paper, to protect ourselves against pain, against
loss, but the papers don't protect us. Neither can a nation. Not yet.
Not as we intend.

17 abril

*This is no dream. Bleeding buckets between my legs as I drive
to the hospital, my future without this child rushes before me. I
try to stop my thoughts: how familiar childlessness is to me; how*

---

interested in cultivating material and voice in their writings that in some way
corresponded to their Indigenous origins.

much simpler it would be; how every corpuscle in my body resists
a return to that state.

When I get to the Kaiser clinic, I go straight into the staff area, looking
for Nurse Eileen. "She's gone for the day," they say.

"But I'm bleeding," I respond. And then I hear her voice.

"Cherríe, is that you?" She enters the room, her round, freckled
face wrinkling into a frown.

When I see her, I am no woman, no future, no thought. I am
all present, all girl-child with baby, and I cry to her, "I'm bleeding."
She rushes me into an examination room and feels for the baby with
groping hands. At that point of contact, I feel my baby move up to
meet her open palms. I know my baby is whole and complete inside.
No miscarriage, the heavy bleeding due to polyps sloughing off from
the cervix.

Since the bleeding—how to describe it? I am homebound and,
ironically, read daily of Maya ritual bloodletting, of shamans
and diviners. I remain ever awed by the fragility of the life inside
me, or maybe it is only I who am fragile.

At each threat to my pregnancy, the baby remains sólido,
intacto. His heartbeat growing in resonance, conviction, full
human-beingness. What relief to hear it beating without distur-
bance next to my frantically beating heart as Nurse Eileen put
the heart monitor to my womb.

I have no control over this vulnerability. I tell Myrtha it is
so hard to want something so bad and to feel that this destiny of
mother and child is truly out of my hands, truly a gift from the
cosmos. I am here to receive it, but I cannot cling to it any more
than I can predict the nature of the son I will have. I keep think-

ing he is his own soul, so much so that at times I forget my own role in shaping him.

My friends remind me. "You will make a wonderful mother," they say. Some have even said how lucky Rafael Angel will be to have me as his mother. And this shocks me each time in the hearing. He is all gift to me. But they tell me that I, also, am a gift to my son.

25 abril

I return from the Medicine Ceremony at Bear Camp. I look for an opening of understanding about my experience there: thirty hours without sleep; the preference given to males throughout la ceremonia—they, the firekeepers, the pipe-carriers, the jefes.

Lying on my bed, the afternoon sun spills over the bedspread and I sleep heavily. When I awaken, I am convinced that there is some ritual of closing I still need to perform. I rise, wash all my clothes, clean my car of earth and mud, my hair and body of smoke, fire, and fatigue.

This writing is part of that closing—that opening, that continuance of what touched me somehow, unwittingly, in these last days of pure offering. Not that my spirit was pure, only that there was no other way to understand the weekend, except to see it as an ofrenda. All was discomfort, working when what I needed was rest, waiting on men (which I found irritating), the intensity of the heat from the sweat lodge (this I wanted), the endless hours of sitting in ceremony, unable to stretch my cramped legs, my spasming back, fighting back a constant call to sleep.

But there were revelations minute by minute. During la ceremonia, as others suffered separation around me, I did not feel alone. Holding my womb, I rocked and rocked, and my son

and I spoke secrets to each other in the circle of the fire. I may
never feel this unalone again, I thought. I prayed and dozed off
into mundane dreams of steak dinners and other small cravings,
then would awaken to pray some more. I prayed that I would
learn how to raise a male child well, that the wounds men have
inflicted onto me, even in their absence, would not poison me
against my son.

I did not have the histories so many of the folks present at
the ceremony claimed: drug abuse, poverty, violent relationships.
"Skid row," one man announced. My battles, challenges, have
always been more invisible. But it is with that history and this
baby inside that I proceed. I ask for light. I thank the spirit for
what has already been freely given.

> Son to his mother at the ceremony:
> "You can lead a horse to water.
> You have led me to the river.
> It's up to me if I'm gonna drink."

There is no closure, only this beginning—my return to Heart
of the Earth with new eyes, my return to Ellen with renewed
understanding. I have this life inside me to thank for the generosity his presence has brought to our relationship. Seeing Ellen's
goodness to me in my pregnancy has opened my heart to her in a
way I sense cannot be reversed. She has allowed me to depend on
her. And, for the first time in my life, I do.

27 abril

Last week, Cesar Chavez died. I cut the grainy newsprint photo
from the already yellowing daily paper. The caption reads: "He
grew up in tar-paper shacks." It is a sad picture: Cesar's forced

half-smile, eyes looking off to the side hooded by aging indio eye-lids, a full head of near-white hair. He is not wholly present in the photo, his heart somewhere else. It shows. I tape the image onto the white wooden wall behind my altar and notice Audre's photo beneath it: her arms outstretched in a communal embrace, her full body draped in West African cloth. She has a radiant smile.

I don't know if Audre and Cesar ever met each other, but between them the story of my own political history as a Chicana and a lesbian is told. A decade ago, Audre and I each left New York and drifted apart. Nothing separated us really, except the calling of our own topography of return. I to my homeland in California—the land of Cesar's movement—and Audre—to her island in the Caribbean.

Since Audre's passing, I've begun to try and speak to her again. It is easier now, the geographical distance no longer of consequence.* It is also easier, I think, because the living always presume the wisdom of those who have passed on, their infinite capacity for understanding, their generosity of spirit. Audre: the first ancestor of my own lesbian of color tradition.

Tell me about freedom now, sister-poet. Teach me.

In Audre and Cesar's passing—the proximity of their deaths to each other—I wonder about leadership. Who is there to replace them?

Cesar died in his sleep, a tired man. In conversation with a friend, she tells me she fears he died of a broken heart. We'll never know. He died suddenly, after thirty years of lucha and no

---

* During my years in New York City (1981–85), Audre Lorde and I became dear friends and great collaborators as founding collective members of Kitchen Table—Women of Color Press. I miss her terribly.

re-emerging movimiento on the horizon. I remember reading, years ago, about Emma Goldman's death in the 1930s, how after a lifetime of devoted anarchism, the woman died watching fascism take root in Europe. She, too, may have died of a broken heart. But not Audre. She died, utterly loved internationally, leaving a movement in her wake.

28 mayo

A full month since I've last written. I dream that Ellen and I are at a botánica. The walls are lined with jars of herbs and medicines from floorboard to ceiling. I don't know what our illness is, or the remedy. I do not feel ill. A beautiful boy of about nine approaches. He is the son of a friend. We say her name in greeting him. He is the essence of life itself—a beautiful brown face, huge eyes, thick dark hair. He exudes a genuine kindness. I wonder, upon waking—is he my son?

30 mayo

I can't write sitting up in bed anymore. My belly's too big. The baby moves around constantly now, especially when I am resting or sitting still. He is a fish inside me, flapping his tail, gulping down the waters of my womb. He is pure animal, nothing human about these sensations. They are the animal I am when I make love, am hungry, move my bowels, fall into a deep unconscious sleep.

Hours ago, Dorothy was here with her nine-month-old baby and her lover. We ate well, conversed lightly, the baby drawing most of our attention. Dorothy spoke briefly of her new novel. Mostly we spoke of the business of writing—the success of Bastard after so many years of hand-to-mouth subsistence, eking out the time and means to write. *

---

* Dorothy Allison's *Bastard Out of Carolina*, published in 1992.

As we spoke, the idea of writing a novel came back to me. Suddenly this baby due, and I realize the vulnerability I feel with my writing career as a playwright and poet; how little money it earns, how hard it is to promote the work. But beyond the financial concerns, I long for that kind of extended involvement in a work. I think, What pleasure to immerse oneself in a single story for a long long time! *I always have the sense that my writing is incomplete somehow—the poems, the plays, the essays striving at something not wholly realized. Maybe the novel would allow me that space to explore the deepest concerns. Thoroughly. I don't know. I write theoretically here when the urge is simply to create. My body now taking on the full shape of creation does not lessen my need for art.*

5 junio

What is sex or prayer (I don't know which) is the spring's sunlight descending into the cooling goldenrod hills. I watch it retreat, starting my bath in the evening light, finishing in darkness. I watch my womb grow, watch the sudden transformation of my body like some holy miracle. I try to reach somewhere wounded and orphaned inside of me and bring this sudden image of my queer womanhood into view: I, the object of my own lesbian, woman-hungry eyes. I, a mama, too, like all the mamas I have longed for and loved.

11 junio / New York City

Here again, to work on yet another draft of Heart of the Earth. *I can't write now because I need to keep my feet up. They have swollen into Flintstone feet in this New York heat, and my hands grow quickly numb holding up this book and pen in the air over my belly. All I am waiting for is to escape this heat, to be rejoined with Ellen at her mother's house on the Cape. To rest.*

18 junio / Cape Cod

As it turns out, it is a humble house, not how I imagined the Cape from Hollywood movies—its dramatic gable architecture, its wealth. No, this is not the Kennedys' Hyannis Port nor Martha's Vineyard. Just the house of a working-class grandma with a mill-town Massachusetts accent. I am somehow relieved by this.

I awaken this morning as an expectant mother, worrying. I don't know if it is the pregnancy or allergies again that cause me to want so much sleep. I take two-hour naps, stay up till midnight, sleep again till 10:00 a.m. The baby greets me with bolder movement each day. I feel him now just to the right of my navel. I dream his future face nightly. I feel a slight muscle spasm in the left side of my neck and imagine my baby has traveled up there, stirring everywhere throughout my body. Hormones. I cry freely and without will or censor.

Last night I went to bed weepy-eyed. Ellen, her mother, and I had just seen a show about transgender people. Since the featured trans woman started out heterosexual, I suggested that her sexuality (attraction to women) will remain the same after her operation and she will become a lesbian. Ellen's mother is mind-boggled.

"But they made her a vagina with feeling. After all that, how could she still want to be with a woman?"

I respond, "I have a vagina with feeling, and I want to be with a woman."

She goes silent.

Later when Ellen comes into the room, we argue about numbers: what percentage of transgender folk become straight, what relationship sexuality has to transgender identity. The debate is not the point. I am hurt by her mother's response. She is not being mean nor truly insensitive—my mother would unwittingly have said (or at least thought) the same. But I wonder how it is that although Ellen and I are present as partners every day in front of her mother, and at night Ellen and I make a purposeful and impassioned love, that in her mom's mind, sex has to be with a penis.

Ellen misunderstands my sadness, my hormone-induced tears. She complains of my "man-hating," my dick-centered resentment (envy). I go to sleep wallowing in my queer sense of isolation, alienation even from my lesbian lover.

She's a femme, I think. She doesn't really understand.

19 junio

Ellen tells me daily how much more feminine I look. I see it, too: my hair longer than it's been in fifteen years, my hips and thighs and breasts rounding from this pregnancy, the softening taking place throughout my body, the tears. I like it and yet in bed I feel a strong urge to reassert my butchness, myself as a love-maker.

But the heart . . . it opens almost effortlessly. I feel closer to Ellen than ever. I tell her how frightening that can be for me, that nakedness. "We are so different," she responds. It is a statement of faithfulness, I know, when it is that face-to-face nakedness she craves. And I have faith too, although I cry.

I cry because I know this is another step into a deepening between us, the terrain of which is as unfamiliar as this baby. After four years, how does one continue loving? What does it look like?

21 junio

Summer solstice finds the Cape, a heavy, hot, grey cloud pressing down upon its grey citizens. But there is an unparalleled beauty here. It lies in the waveless steel-tinted sea. Its endlessness.

Yesterday Ellen and I went to the beach.

We stop first at the bathroom. She is in the stall next to me. I very methodically cut strips of toilet paper to line the toilet seat before I sit (the way my mother taught me as a child). Just as I start to sit down, I look up and see Ellen has been watching me, her head peeking over the stall wall. In jest, she has put on a monster's face, sticking out her tongue, twisting her mouth, and rolling her eyes up into her head. I am so startled that, even as she laughs, I break out into deep sobs. Where the fear comes from, I don't know. I am amazed and relieved by the tears, how completely I experience everything these days. Later, when Ellen inadvertently bumps a tree in the parking lot as she backs the car out, I scream at her. I am primordial protection. I am afraid that my baby has been jolted, afraid of what could have happened with a harder knock, a crash. I cry.

I have a vague sense that I dreamed last night I had given birth prematurely. Again. He is only in his sixth month, and I worry that his lungs are not yet fully developed enough to survive on his own.

22 junio

But after you hear the story,
you and the others prepare by the new moon
to rise up against the slave masters.

—Leslie Marmon Silko, *Almanac of the Dead*

I lose the thread, the purpose of the writing until I am reminded by Marmon Silko's words—that a story can cause revolt. That is my sole purpose. Is it hubris to think I might write those kinds of works? Stories to agitate, stories to remind us of what has been forgotten?

These days I doubt my capacity to do that. I wonder if that feeling ever goes away in the life of the writer. In the realm of my self-doubt, the world becomes unbearably small, as small as my pitiful ego. But when I imagine I can speak with the voice of others—that others can speak through me—how wide and hopeful the project of writing becomes again.

A boy of about nine walks by this Cape Cod window. He carries a violin case. He must have an 8:00 a.m. Friday appointment down the dead-end street. He looks neither eager nor sullen about going, only obligatory. Minutes later, the little boy returns by the same path, passes by the window again. He looks fatter upon his return, thoroughly irritated. He swings his free arm heavy with a child's unempowered resentment. Wrong day? Wrong time? Nobody home?

These journal entries are my meager attempts to keep the pen flowing, to discover the next step en la jornada. My writer's road is now open. Heart of the Earth, *on tour in upstate New York, and the play collection off to its publisher.** *I feel empty of stories, empty of ideas, words, images, impulses. The creative juices used to fuel this baby's development only make my hunger for writing stronger. I shape these letters onto the page as tiny steps in a dance circling, circling, circling until I arrive at the heartbeat, a pulse, a place from which the writing stirs new life.*

---

* *Heroes and Saints & Other Plays* (Albuquerque, NM: West End Press, 1994).

30 junio / Kaiser Hospital, Hollywood

I watch the heart monitor obsessively. It is everything to me. Like religion. All that matters is the stress-free beating of my baby's heart, his kicking signs of life, the steady unwavering pattern of the monitor printout indicating no contractions. But I am awakened at 2:00 a.m., a routine check, and am told contractions are seven to eight minutes apart. My world shrinks to the parameter of my thirsty womb as I beg my baby to stay put there, hold on, cling to me, incubating as long as possible. This is not a dream.

Twenty-seven weeks is so damn young.

My water broke the day before I was due to return to San Francisco. The date was June 27, 1993.

Following my stay in Cape Cod, I had flown to Los Angeles for a brief visit with my family, knowing I probably wouldn't see them again until after the baby's birth in late September. I had gone with my sister's family to Huntington Beach the night before for an evening bonfire, but my brother-in-law had other plans. He wanted to talk, he told me. He actually said he wanted to "find closure," a therapeutic term he had acquired during the three brief visits of couples' counseling he had done with my sister. He had to discuss their impending divorce, bare his soul, and so off we walked down the beach for what seemed like miles. As my brother-in-law talked and talked and talked, I knew this one-way conversation had nothing to do with me and everything to do with him and the image he was working on creating of himself as a responsible, sensitive kind of guy: father, husband, ex-husband, ex-brother-in-law.

The day before that, my sister had pressed on—"Let's go to another mall"—in earnest search of (more) baby paraphernalia. I knew I was slowly beginning to lose it physically, emotionally. *Wait until I get home,* I thought. *This is the least I can do for people who need me.*

But the baby wouldn't wait.

The next morning at my parents' house in San Gabriel, suddenly feeling overwhelmingly tired, I excuse myself from the breakfast table. My parents both turn their faces up to me and away from their morning eggs. I had to go back to bed, I told them, just for an hour or so. And they agree rest is what I need.

The exhaustion is so sudden, so bottomless as I drag myself off to the closet-sized room that was once my brother's bedroom. The phone rings, just as I feel the rush of warm water bathe my thighs. I know it is Ellen. I reach over to the phone, lift up the receiver. "My water just broke," I cry. I am not seven months pregnant.

She catches the first flight out of Boston.

After a series of phone calls—between my mom and Ellen, Ellen and Kaiser, between LA and San Francisco and Cape Cod, Ellen frantically trying to get the best medical advice for me from three thousand miles away—my parents manage to get me an appointment with a private obstetrician. They lay me carefully onto the back seat of the family car, and when we arrive at the clinic, my father finds a wheelchair to get me up to the third floor. In retrospect, I see now I should have gone directly to emergency, and that's what the doctor says minutes after the sonogram showed my womb virtually empty of amniotic fluid. Merely a small dark pool of liquid remained, not nearly enough to keep a baby afloat. I am horrified as I study the sonogram monitor. My mother stands next to me. "The baby's fine," she says, not fully understanding the signs. I tell her, "It's not good, Mamá. He's too little to be born now!"

The ambulance drive from the clinic in Pasadena to Hollywood Kaiser is interminable. Flat on the gurney, I try to read the route from the shape of streetlights overhead, the curve of freeway interchanges, the tops of palm and sycamore trees lining the backstreets we travel. My mother is in the front seat with the driver. My father will meet us there in his own car. I make idle chit-chat with the salvadoreño paramedic, but my mouth has dropped somewhere into my womb and I sing only one real song: *Hang on, mijito. Stay inside me, please stay inside me.*

As we arrive at the hospital, I am rolled on the same gurney directly into the labor room. If the baby doesn't come in twenty-four hours, the doctors tell me, he can stay in my womb for weeks, maybe months, even without the fluid. The objective is to keep the baby inside me for as long as possible. I am to remain flat on my back and in the hospital until this baby is born. The next day, Ellen arrives. I hadn't realized how much I was needing her until our eyes meet. Her face is the mirror of tenderness, of recognition I have been waiting for. She rushes to me. My parents graciously leave us alone, and I cry my child's heart out.

After the initial crisis, it appears that Rafael has decided to hold on for a while. I have had no contractions for twenty-four hours, so I am moved into the maternity ward to homestead. At twenty-seven weeks' gestation, they tell us, the baby's lungs are not strong enough to breathe on their own. Ellen has already found two books on premature births. She studies them. She explains the risks to me, editing out the worst potential parts of the scenario. Thirty-two weeks is our goal. At thirty-two weeks' gestation, the baby can breathe well on his own, the heart duct that is connected to the lungs has closed, and the baby will be small but quite whole and out of danger.

Thirty-two weeks never come, nor does a full twenty-eight. For the next six days the baby remains inside me. My family visits me with vigilance, Ellen ever-faithful at my bedside. With every change in my body temperature, every increase or decrease in contractions,

I am taken from the maternity ward to delivery and back again. I am visited by a revolving door of neonatalists, residents, interns, nurses, and nurse's aides, but no one seems to be able to clearly answer my questions: How did this happen? I had no infection, no trauma to my womb. What are my baby's chances for survival and a healthy life? One incident I remember vividly is being told off-handedly by a resident (at least fifteen years younger than I), as she did a routine check, that if my baby were to be born right then, it would have a 25 percent chance for survival. Not true, I learn later, but in seconds my temperature shoots up and I am put back on a heart monitor.

3 julio

Rafael Angel is born 3:05 p.m. Full moon.

I am speechless—my child somehow exactly as I had imagined him. This gift, this messenger child, who could not wait to enter me, to enter this world. I sleep now to dream of him, dreaming down the hall, a two-pound-six-ounce milagrito, mi bebé.

The intensive part of the labor is short: four hours. I have the nurses call Ellen that morning of July third, somehow knowing today would be the day. The doctors still have given me no clear sense of what a twenty-eight-week birth means for my baby's health. I try to push that worry out of my mind; I think only of a safe delivery.

The night before, Ellen had stayed with me in the labor room until the early hours of the morning. The contractions were strong enough to feel, but not so strong that I couldn't fall asleep. I finally send her home (my parents' home) for some rest. At 7:00 a.m. I am awake. The contractions are stronger now, still not severe enough to be concerned, I think. I have the nurses call Ellen. "Ask her to be here by eleven," I say. Somehow the message gets confused. My mother receives the call, doesn't want to disturb Ellen sleeping, but can't figure out if there is a reason to worry. She calls my sister. At eleven, Ellen and Jo Ann both magically arrive, independent of one another. That's all I need. Once my sister and Ellen are here, I know I'm in good hands.

Needless to say, Ellen and I never took the natural childbirth classes. Those were to be reserved for those lazy August months when I'd have nothing better to do. My sister, however, was a virtual pro at Lamaze, having given birth to four healthy babies with that method. So, minutes after Jo Ann arrives, she is grilling me with questions about my symptoms. "Where do you feel the pain? How far apart are the contractions?" And Ellen is flipping frantically through childbirth books, trying to read about what's going to happen minutes before it's happening. But they make a marvelous delivery team. As the pains increase in intensity, Ellen (per Jo Ann's instructions) pushes on my lower back to relieve some of the pain. I have never appreciated Ellen's physical strength as I did that day. No lightweight lover for me, the girl is pure power.

A few hours later, my parents arrive with my Auntie Eva. They are all dressed up y perfumadas, coming for a casual hospital visit. Try as I might, I cannot keep face. I am in the throes of labor, and my sister gracefully tells them this is not such a good time for the visit. She'll call when we know anything more. They leave the hospital, a bit disoriented, none of us knowing I would deliver in the next hour.

How could we know? This is my first baby, and during a full week of being taken in and out of the labor room, I had heard my neighbor-laborers screaming at the top of their lungs.

"Ay, Mamacita!"

"Give me some damn drugs!"

"No! No! No!"

So, I figure that whatever pain I got going (which was the fiercest physical pain I had ever experienced), it has to get worse and I am trying to conserve what energy I have for the long haul. My sister keeps assuring me that a big mouth doesn't necessarily mean bigger pain. Still, I hang on, politely breathing as Jo Ann instructs me, pushing out air in long drags, then short rhythmic puffs. All the while, Ellen keeps pressing on my back for a moment of blessed relief, then rushes back to her birthing books. In the meantime, Jo Ann jots down in a little notepad how close the contractions are coming.

Now the contractions are one on top of the other and virtually unbearable. My sister suggests I get up on all fours to relieve the pressure on my lower back where the pain is the most severe. The moment I do, I feel a revolution occur in my womb, the pain taking a full somersault inside of me, dropping down into what feels like my bowels. (Thinking about it later, I realize that that one move may have saved me hours of labor.) I fall back onto my back, feel the urge to defecate, tell them so. Jo Ann says, "That's the *baby*."

Ellen rushes out to get a doctor. The staff has virtually ignored us for the last three hours since every time they checked the monitor, it wasn't reading the contractions as intensely as I was experiencing them. The doctor wastes no time in coming. Since the time my water broke, seven days earlier, I had not been examined vaginally, for fear of infection. No one, therefore, had checked the dilation of my cervix throughout the labor. As the young Asian American resident is opening my legs, I glance at the clock above her head. Three o'clock. Her hand moves up inside me. "I can feel the head," she says. "Get her into the delivery room."

Now I know what that statement means for a premature baby. Within five minutes, the on-call staff at the Intensive Care Nursery— the neonatalist, the respiratory therapist, the ICN nurse—will meet us in delivery. Ellen and Jo Ann have disappeared. Next time I see them, they are standing on each side of me, wearing pale pink surgical gowns and masks. The doctor tells me to push. And I do. Grabbing my sister's hand on my left side, my Ellen's on the right, I push with everything I've got. I hear them prompting me on, everybody approving. "Good, good, good." I push. "That's it, he's coming. Go on." I push. "There he is, one more." Ellen tells me she can see him. Then the doctor's voice is urgent. "Stop. Don't push. Hold back." I don't know why. My vagina is pure fire, a horrible burning. When everything in me wants to push him all the way out, they tell me to stop. But it is the cord, the cord is wrapped around his neck. The doctor remains very calm, cuts the baby free. Then I let go and let him spill out of me.

Relief; my body is engulfed in a pleasure, an animal pleasure, a pulsing, an aliveness like nothing I've known. I am a girl and a woman and an animal, y estoy temblando like the best of sex, the best of being thoroughly entered and spent. They don't bring the baby to my belly as they do in the movies. I see out of the corner of my eye a circle of masked strangers around him. They, too, are dressed in pink. I am afraid to look, afraid to know how my baby looks. *Is he well? Is he breathing?* A final push and the afterbirth spills out of me. I want to keep the cord, bury it somewhere, somewhere far away from this hospital. How is my baby?

Then Ellen ventures over to him, breaking that tight circle of urgent latexed hands and plastic tubes and blinking monitors. I hear her from the distance, a mere distance of five feet or so, which seems so far away from me. She says, "He has an indio nose." And I cry from relief now. I cry and laugh and tremble with the joy of his birthing. It was the best thing to say. I know he is okay or else she would have said something else. He is okay, alive, whole, born. They rush him out of the delivery room into Intensive Care. I still haven't seen his face.

After a few hours of recovery, Ellen and my sister take me over to the ICN. I must admit, I am afraid to go, afraid to see this being whose face my lover has seen but not I, not yet. But when I do see him, he is a miniature of all I understand of beauty. He is the tiniest creature I have ever seen. His skin hangs off of him como un viejito, and there is a thin veil of dark hair coating his body. He is the most beautiful little monkey in the world. I am not shocked to see him. He looks just as I have imagined him, but his fragility is almost unfathomable. How do I protect him from so far away?

That night, after Ellen leaves, I consider what has brought me, now us, to this place in time. In a way, the most natural thing in the world was to give birth here in Los Angeles, among my blood familia. I knew as I held Ellen's and my sister's hands in the grip of labor that this was what I understood as hogar, sustenance; that this is how a woman should always give birth, surrounded by women. And how lucky I am to be a lesbian, to have it all—mother, sister, lover—that family of women to see me into motherhood.

I couldn't help but think we had willed it in some way—he and I—to give birth to Rafael Angel in the City of the Angels.

II

WAITING IN THE WINGS

POSTPARTUM, 1993

I've never before experienced the feeling
of having to physically keep Death away,
as if he would actually come in the door
if I let down my guard for an instant.

—Paul Monette, *Borrowed Time*

Nothing will ever be the same.

I knew our lives would be changed by the arrival of this baby, but the manner of his arrival is as nothing I have known in my life, feeling so awestruck by every moment—Rafaelito's push toward life. I am afraid to write of these times, afraid somehow language will lessen what I know.

7 julio / San Gabriel

I am out of the hospital, and as I fight off the traces of a cold, I focus on nothing else but purifying myself so that when Rafaelito begins to draw from my milk tomorrow, it will fortify him, sustain him as his life-struggle sustains me. This child is no stranger to me—possibly because he looks now as he will look eighty years from now, an old man, I already gone. I see in him my mother's aging forehead, my own collapsing chin (once perfectly delineated), the blurring ancient eyes of my grandmother in the years just before her death at ninety-six. But my son's life lies before him, and each day the ancientness will obscure itself in ounces of baby fat. He will carry this knowledge of this closeness to death, the other side of life, as a great secret inside of him.

Today I do not visit him. I take the day to recuperate, but every time I close my eyes, he is visible right behind my eyelids, an image pressed upon my memory, my sleeping and waking life. My mind does not always serve as my friend. My heart, yes. In that place resides a seamless connection between my baby's essence beating inside those incubator walls and my milk-hard-breasted body. I struggle to overcome this constant fear and anxiety in the effort to discover a deep and unwavering faith in his survival, his fruitfulness, his life.

8 julio

My faith has been challenged. Faith in what? The benevolence of the universe? To whom do I pray? To the dispassionate face of the Indian Virgen who must know something of what I suffer—she who bore a son, who lost a son? To the broken body of an Aztec lunar goddess that I witnessed whole and womanly two Mexican summers past? Is it her strength—la fuerza de Coyolxauhqui—I draw from, a female power potent enough to eclipse the sun? Or is it the Califas ocean, swelling into a rage yet tender enough to sustain a child's blue balloon afloat for hours? I follow the balloon with my eyes as it dances at the precipice of the breaking waves. These are the ruminations of a fully grown, fully unfearful woman. That is not me.

At forty, I feel myself respond to the crisis of Rafaelito's sudden entrance into this world as I did as a child of eight, fearing my mother's death. At eight, I prayed endlessly all night long as my mother lay in a hospital bed some fifteen miles away. I dug a crater into the inside of my elbow with nervous nails, scratching scratching scratching. I worried. I worried for her life. I grew superstitious, feared the wrong set of prayers, a forgotten passage, a misdirected look at a plaster saint could mean her death. I prayed and feared always God's punishment, God's closed ears and heart. I kept my sister up at night. I cried.

Today my mother said to me, "Remember, hija, it was your prayers that got me out of the hospital." She, too, thought of the

child I was thirty-two years ago. Now I see faith is not so easy to
secure. I am still superstitious as I pour some of my breast milk
as offering into the garden earth. I fear the wrong gesture, the
wrong words might offend those ever-heartless gods. I take the
chance anyway, watering the garden with my body's milk. I pray
as I pour—for life, for my son's life.

As I watch Rafaelito grow stronger and healthier each day, I
can't make sense of my blessing in the face of the ailing babies next
to him, barely clinging to life, hooked up to respirators and IVs.

When my mother and I go to Sears to buy nursing bras and
newborn infant wear (clothes Rafaelito cannot possibly fit into
for months), she tells the young Chicana cashier about my pree-
mie baby boy. The cashier tells us of her brother, also born premature, now thirteen with a cleft palate and seizures. "He's only
grown up to here." She measures the air, stopping at her elbow.

I fear hearing her speak of it, fear bad omens lying dormant
in strangers' anecdotes. My mother confesses the same fear to me.
Coming out of the store into the low-hanging LA smog she says,
"When I was pregnant, I thought it wasn't good to even look at a
deformed child."*

My deepest faith has been challenged. I have never been so
close to and so afraid of death as I have been with the emergence
of my son into the world. How does one have faith when one is
consumed by fear? I have felt this way since the moment my water
broke without warning ten days ago. But as I held him for the first
time today, my hand wrapping fully around the small bird weight

---

* My mother's words feel very old and Mexican to me, which is why it is included
here; how I have inherited what appears to be "superstition," but perhaps is
something else, deeper, simply protective and maternal. The fear reflected here is
not intended to diminish the value of our children in anyway disabled.

of his head, all was life. He is thoroughly present, his blue-black eyes taking me in. "Sí, soy tu mamá," I say. He is as near to me as when he kicked inside me, and I am filled with hope and promise for our lives together. Maybe Rafaelito will bring to me a more profound way of believing. Rafael: "the healing power of God," I remember the phrase. Maybe he is my teacher.

9 julio

I dream that my son has been born but is not fully human in form yet. He is a kind of gusanito in the early stages of development. How gratified I was to awaken to the memory of his perfectly human face staring back at me from my arms.

In another dream, I am to attend some kind of gathering of women, a kind of retreat. When I arrive, I am shocked to see mostly white women dressed in ethnic fabrics. I can't keep face. I don't want to be here. I want to find my sister. I cry and cry and want to return only to my baby's side. I can think of nothing else.

Later, in the same dream, I am on the phone debating with a man, then a woman, over their rights to a piece of my writing. "I don't give a damn," I tell them. "I'll return the payment to you. Don't use my work." I cry to my mother, "I care about nothing but this baby." She understands.

About five days after Rafa's birth, Ellen goes home to San Francisco to "get things in order." The plan is that she will return in a week, and that we will spend the summer here in Los Angeles until the baby is well and grown enough to return with us to San Francisco. We will sublet an apartment and move our work south for the time being (at least two to three months, they tell us).

Rafael Angel's condition has been stable so far, his breathing normal, with the occasional bradycardia* when he "forgets" to breathe. The nurses tell us it is normal, his premature system not yet in full operation. I am awed that even the instinct to breathe is not a given. Rafaelito is also too young to suck. For at least the next five weeks he will be fed my breast milk through a tube down his throat. So I pump and label and store my milk in the hospital freezer and in my parents' freezer, transporting it in small ice chests each day to the ICN. As I watch the soft white liquid descend through the tube into his pursed mouth, I tell him, "One day, hijo, te daré el pecho. Ten paciencia." I say this more for myself than him.

14 julio

Rafael is transported by air ambulance to San Francisco Kaiser.
We are not home yet.

I arrive one morning at the ICN to be told, without warning, that Rafaelito is stable enough to be transferred to San Francisco Kaiser.

"Is it safe?" I ask.

Yes, they tell me, explaining that a nurse, a doctor, and a respiratory therapist will fly down from San Francisco to travel with him. I call Ellen right away, tell her, "Don't bother coming down. We're coming home."

The hospital plane is waiting as we pull up in the ambulance. Rafaelito is rolled aboard in a compact incubator with all the necessary accoutrements: heart monitor, oxygen saturation monitor, IV in place, respirator ready to go just in case. Nurse Bobbie from San Francisco Kaiser is a mixed blessing, cracking jokes the entire way about "Raf-ee-el" already being a jetsetter, playing stewardess as she passes out plastic-wrapped sandwiches and beverages. She relieves me of

---

* Excessively slow heartbeat rate

some of my anxiety, but is a bit more blonde-cheerleader than my mood. Still, when she asks if Ellen will be there to meet me, referring to her by name, my heart opens to her. She's read the report, I think. She knows we are lesbians, and I am relieved that we will have at least one emissary at this new hospital. One less thing to explain.

The doctor, a thin, bearded neonatalist, has little to say to me throughout the trip. As I gaze out the porthole window, the view moving from farmland to forest, I hear him making copious notes next to me, his pen scratching against the clipboard. I glance over to the report on his lap, spot the words "artificial insemination." Everybody knows my business, I think, and I remember how un-artificial that moment felt to me. Then I ask him, "So, what do you think, Doctor? How's the baby gonna do?"

He answers, almost disappointed, "Oh, this baby's not even a challenge." I think that is supposed to encourage me, but weeks later, when Rafael is being taken into surgery barely clinging to life, I want to ask him, "Challenge enough for you now, Doc?"

19 julio / San Francisco

This time is a subtle study in nonaction
as a way of attaining real meaning in your life.

—I-Ching

No truer words. I am in the hospital cafeteria again. These days are the hard days. Rafaelito is back on a ventilator, blood transfusion yesterday, twenty-four hours nonstop bradycardia. Today he is stable but exhausted. I am exhausted, too, have never lived like this before. It takes great effort to move this pen across the page in an attempt to document some thread of what I am/we

*are experiencing. To document my son's survival. "Mi guerrero,"
I call him. My warrior boy.*

*Tede died yesterday. Without his knowing he has been an inti-
mate part of Rafaelito's life. Tede writing me of angels, never
knowing I held one with folded wings inside of me; that I chose
Angel for Rafaelito's second name. Hearing that Tede had AIDS
so close to the news of Rafael's sex, I wonder—is there a kind of
queer balance to this birthing and dying? Lesbians giving life to
males, while our queer brothers pass on? He is the child of queers,
our queer and blessed family, laughing with Ricardo and Ellen
sitting on the bed next to me after the insemination. We just
laughed and laughed.*

*Rafaelito came to me effortlessly, our first try at conception. He
was, literally, waiting in the wings—angel wings—waiting for me
to finally decide to call him to this earth. But now I see Rafaelito is
not so easily won. He enters this life with a delicate, deep strength,
as a living reminder of the precariousness of our lives. I breathe
through the isolette, call to him, to me, to us, to life. "Rafaelito,
Rafaelito, quédate aquí, hijo, con nosotros. Tu familia te espera."
I call him over to this side.*

It is hard to write, harder yet to pray.

*I am now in the Intensive Care Nursery. "Rafaelito, se ve tan
pálido." They tell me not to touch him today, to let him rest, but I
want him to know I am here. I do not touch. I watch. I watch his
small ribcage rise and fall, sometimes with such great effort. Then
when his chest is still, I search the monitors frantically, always*

in momentary panic that mi hijo may have forgotten again to breathe. At this hour of the late afternoon, his chest appears almost transparent. Ellen arrives.

20 julio

Ellen called the hospital this morning to inquire about the baby, having to put up with the usual deterrents: "Who are you?" The receptionist hears no male voice on the line, but a woman, my lover, seeking to know about our son.

"Read the damn chart," Ellen snaps back. "I'm the co-mother." "Co-mother"—a concept about which even San Francisco hospitals haven't a clue. I cannot comfort Ellen much when she is bruised by the hospital's ignorance.

I hear only her telling me Rafaelito has had more "bradys." "How many?" I want to know and do not want to know and suffer that I am not there with him at this moment and suffer that I also can hardly bear to see him struggle so to breathe. And still we don't know what's wrong with him.

Ellen and I will split shift tomorrow: me, in the day, she, in the evening, so he won't be left alone without us. We draw comfort seeing him together, but it seems there is little room for comfort these days. I learn the lessons of motherhood daily. There are no guarantees, only faith. But what is there to believe in other than simply Rafaelito was destined to come into this life and share it for a time with us? How I want that time to be full and long and rich. How desperately I want his survival as I have wanted nothing before in my life. I pray for this as minute-by-minute Rafaelito struggles simply to remember to breathe.

21 julio

"Something's not right with this kid, Doc."

Nurse Rose insists and persists. Ellen stands sentinel next to her. She, too, insists on answers. Now. What is happening to our child? *I sit by Rafaelito's isolette, motionless. I am riveted to the chair. I have no voice, only that same silent mantra inside my heart. "Quédate aquí, hijo. Quédate." The monitors indicating bradycardias are going off dozens of times a minute now. And with each alarm, I feel my heart jolt. With each jolt, Ellen and I lock eyes.*

Are we losing our son?

The doctor on call is not responding: that same nonchalant neonatalist I met on that hospital plane one week ago. "Something is not right with this kid, Doc," Rose insists. Again. At first, they think it is pneumonia. They take a chest X-ray. Nada. An inaccurate image. They take another and, by chance, a partial picture of the intestines can be seen. There is a small dark spot.

24 julio

I didn't write when the days were the worst, when they rolled his tiny isolette down the corridor into surgery and Rafaelito followed our sad gaze (a calm recognition in his eyes) until he was out of sight. I didn't write when they told us the hardest words to hear, "If it is too late, we'll just close him up again." Our baby had contracted NEC, the thing we most feared, an infection that literally eats up the intestine, deadly among many preemies.*

In the waiting room one floor below surgery, we wait for some word. Ricardo has just left, or rather we sent him away, somehow knowing

---

* Necrotizing enterocolitis.

Ellen and I needed to be alone in this, needed to find a private way to stave off this baby's passing. I have brought a rosary, the wooden one given to me by my mother. Ellen and I wrap ourselves up together in the deep vinyl lounge chair; we hold each other and pray. "Dios te salve, Maria . . ."

> You were there, weren't you, Tede? Irish and ancestor. Our queer recently born ancestor with all the dead Mexican relatives we remembered and invoked. Abuelita, who always asked me, "¿Cuando te vas a casar, hija? Necesitas familia." While my family held me in her lion arms and my son had his guts cut open on the floor just above our heads.

In the midst of our prayer, I suddenly realize, so profoundly, that my tightest hold against death cannot keep Rafaelito here. The holding itself is what Rafaelito does not need. He needs to be free to decide: to stay or to leave. Oh, how I hoped he would stay, but I couldn't make it happen. I only knew my clinging so tightly to my son's waning life could surely crush him and all the heart I had; and there would be no heart left to either mourn or raise a son. I can't explain the feeling, that moment of saying to Ellen, against every instinct in me, "We gotta let go." Wasn't it our vigilance that was keeping him here? In the letting go might he not slip from us completely? That was the risk, for what did we two know of death in this most intimate way?

"Si es tu voluntad." I find myself saying the unthinkable out loud—"If it is your will"—passing on the decision to powers beyond us. But in that gesture of releasing him, I felt Rafaelito move toward us, toward life.

Forty-five minutes into a three-and-a-half-hour surgery, Nurse Stacey comes in and tells us, "There was a small perforation in the intestine. The surgeons removed only two centimeters and the ileoce-cal valve. He's going to be fine."*

Soon after, my comadre Deborah arrives, packed for survival. She creates an altar on the small lamp table from the holy cards and heal-ing stones she has brought. We don't light the incense, but place the sage next to the burning candle enflaming the face of la Virgen. My rebozo becomes the altar cloth. We give thanks. Estér and Renée show up later. Ellen has called them. "We need some family with us," she said. When Rafaelito is brought back to the ICN, he is a limp yellow doll, a stripped monkey naked under the glare of heat lamps. He is all wound, and he is my son, breathing through a respirator, stable, and so morphined he is feeling no pain. We finally get ourselves out of there.

Tede stays with our child, like an angel.

25 julio

For the first time since Rafaelito's transport to San Francisco, I've taken the day off, feeling a sore throat coming on. I call the nurse on duty. The news is good. All signs promising that Rafael is recov-ering well. I think of nothing, no one, but my baby, even as I wash the rugs, dry the dishes. Oh yes, surely as I pump my breasts, I imagine his miniature mouth opening onto their dark rose tip. I imagine his earliest most earnest seeking. I imagine his return to la madre from whom he was so abruptly separated, me, my womb, that sweet protection. The world outside full of danger.

It is hard to write when there is no fixed me to be. I am not the same. I don't know how to write of death. I read The Tibetan

---

* Rather than reconnecting the intestine where the removal of the dead matter took place, the surgeons give the baby a temporary ileostomy in order to relieve stress on the colon. For the next three months, Rafaelito would be passing stool into a small bag attached to his lower right abdomen.

Book of Living and Dying *and know I am like the majority,*
afraid to even name death, that somehow in the naming it will
surely visit me. And yet I also know that this is the next necessary
step. Rafaelito's close encounter with death, his tenuous hold on
life, his fragile and threatened beginnings, have introduced me to
living with the knowledge of death.

26 julio

My baby's lungs are the size of teardrops, and I am still too afraid
to fully cry.

Now that my son heals himself, is it residual fear that causes
the fire of an unnamed panic to rise up my spine, spill across
the back of my shoulders, flood my heart and close down my
throat without warning? Daily I have watched fear's venom pass
through plastic tubes, in and out of open veins and miniature
organs. I know fear's scent pressed into the industrial detergent
smell of my baby's doll-sized sheets and blankets. We carry its
odorless indifference home with us on our clothes, in our skin.

Susto, es susto.

The oxygen tube will be removed this morning. I pray for Rafaeli-
to's strong lungs.

29 julio

Tonight, I am unable to sleep. I get up, disturbed by what seems
to be again an infection in my system, warding off a sore throat
all week. I have felt off-balance for months now, since the advent
of allergy season. "No one responded," I tell Ellen. Throughout
the last months of pregnancy, no one took my allergies, my sinus
infections seriously. Yet a part of me feels that these infections are

what wore me down, eventually causing the rupture of my membrane, my water breaking. We'll never know for sure.

1 agosto

Again last night we watched Rafaelito's energy wane, watched him recede into his miniature cuerpecito, lie low and await his own renewal: the transfusion of blood, the rush of antibiotics. This morning I call about his condition and revel in the news of his orneriness, his anger at not being fed. "He's kicking up a storm," Nurse Bobbie tells me. "He's mad that we're not feeding him yet." A few hours later, we learn Rafa is finally eating— barely three cc's every two hours. He is on his own steam. And, again, I know my baby will pass through this, regain his health, return to us whole.

It is a return. His early separation was so radical, the wound of which is salved only in the sudden appearance of a droplet of milk at the lip of my tit, the movement of Rafael kicking against my belly as I hold him naked against the skin of my chest. His smell. His smell that grew sweet with the rise of milk inside my breasts, that grew sweeter with the scent of birthing. Even my sister tells me, "I love that smell. I'll never forget that smell," knowing it four times in her life. She didn't mean some baby wrapped in the newborn warmth of a receiving blanket. She meant the thick-membraned blood-smell passing out between a woman's legs at birth and for a full moon's cycle following. I didn't tell her how close the scent came to the shared intimacy of lesbian desire. A mother-smell. A mother-lover smell. Just alive. Just life.

My baby's newborn smell sleeps in every item of tiny clothing—T-shirt, sleeper, knitted cap and booties—I lay out, fold and shape, and prepare for his arrival. The smell holds an innocence like nothing I imagined, only remembered vaguely in my own once-innocence. Ironically, as my baby grows older, he grows more innocent; he becomes more "baby" and less sabio, less viejito, less my mother's aging face and, instead, the seamless face of hopefulness, of a future.

But his hands retain the memory.

Wrinkled, the map of generations come with him.

8 agosto

I saw God in Rafael Angel. In the simple act of will not to die— as if he had the power to choose. Only God got that power, I had thought, until that moment. He was young enough, small enough to remember where he'd come from. He could've chosen to return.

Rafael is my poem; el milagro of what has passed and what will go forward. He is history and future as Tede now knows, as Audre was given the daily reminder of for fifteen years, battling cancer. Through Rafael I have been given the gift of bearing witness to a soul's decision to take hold of an earthly life. We have stood on this side calling to him, "Come join us, hijo. Stay here with us." This time, we know he is going nowhere but into our arms, into the embrace of this worldly existence. He has made a decision that at twenty-eight weeks we didn't know for sure he would make. Now after five weeks on this planet, we know he will remain with us and "live to be a very old man," as Nurse Rose tells us.

Rose has become our "seer" of sorts, bringing in the holy cards of archangels and St. Jude, the Patron of Lost Causes, as well as direc-

tives from her recently passed mother, who, according to Rose, was la
mera curandera croata in Kansas City.

Rose convinces me to make the trip over to the shrine of St.
Jude, a mile or so from Kaiser at St. Dominic's Church. The edifice
is a massive monument to San Francisco's Catholic elite, but inside
I draw comfort from the stale scent of frankincense and the wintry
childhood smell of melting votives. I follow Rose's directions and
make my way up the side aisle to the shrine of St. Jude, ablaze with
white candles. I slip a five into the metal slot, light five candles, and
with each I pray not only for Rafa, but for all the babies and their
ailments I've come to know in the ICN: for Alex, that her sleeping
limbs will awaken; for Nathaniel, that his heart will heal; for Sim-
one, that her eyes will see clear and far; for Freddy with Downs that
his father may learn to love him; and for all the others I've seen, mir-
roring Rafa's own embattled state, one- and two- and three-pound
human animals with swollen brains and strokes and weak hearts and
drug addictions and troubled families, just struggling to hold onto
the little life they got.

Leaving the church, I run into a man asking for change and a
prayer. For some reason, I tell him that my son is sick and in the hospital. He says he had a son once. I give him a twenty. I couldn't help it. I
give him a twenty to ward off death.

15 agosto

*Over six weeks in the hospital since Rafael Angel's birth. Six
weeks. And we may have as much as another six weeks ahead of
us. Ellen and I are beginning to feel the aftershocks of our near-loss
of Rafa. The last four days he struggles against a new infection, a
staph infection, brought on by the IV needle implanted in his chest.
We worry over what could still come in the months ahead.*

I think of little else but him. Ellen tells me I'm obsessed, but I know there is no other response to have. We wear each other down. I hear her cry, but I cannot comfort her. I move about as a nervous child. Fear—its violent rush of adrenaline—grows horribly familiar, and I clean and hammer and fill empty boxes and move furniture and do laundry and wash dishes and dishes with a vengeance. Against whom? Against death? Against its residual poison left in my bloodstream? I drown the taste out with a shot of tequila. I sleep a dreamless dead sleep to fortify myself for the next day.

It was harder than ever to leave Rafael in the hospital yesterday, to be parted from him. Each leave-taking a violent rupture. I return home without my child. Again empty-handed. Ellen and I fight because we are tired and worried and empty-handed. All is an effort, except the spontaneous impulse toward this baby. I am not inside this writing at all in my heart. I am across the city, my face pressed to the steaming plastic glass of Rafaelito's isolette.

17 agosto

Some change has taken place. The garden flourishes, although Ellen battles daily against the onslaught of ants and aphids. Yesterday Rafael Angel looked better than ever, contento, tranquilo. Well-fed, his color took on a richness I hadn't seen since his birth. I put him to my breast, and he lives complete as a life's lesson in the moment of that suck-and-pull-and-rush of liquid filling his mouth and throat, settling full and sweet at the base of his hunger. His hunger, for now, can be satisfied.

21 agosto

I awake at 4:30 a.m. from a dream in which Rafael is suddenly losing weight. He is down to six hundred grams. He won't make

*it. I am beyond shock, beyond fear. Bobbie is the nurse in charge.
She is not alarmed, only acquiescent in a way to his dying. I can't
bear it. No one seems to be responding. He is slipping away. The
feeling recurs, cannot be shaken off. It lies vigilant inside me
throughout all these weeks since his birth: a sense of the inevita-
ble finally coming to pass. Más que miedo, es susto.*

*Writing at this hour (5:15 a.m.), I visualize Rafael Angel in
his isolette in the hospital. I wonder if he is awake now. I realize
as he energetically gains weight that with each gram he moves
closer to his return to me, to us, to his home. I wonder if this
morning's dream provides a lesson grander than predictable plot
lines. With each gram, he also grows less and less dependent, less
mine. He will never be mine and will surely pass away one day,
as inevitably as life predicts it. And I will be already parted from
this body.*

*My parents are here to visit. A good visit. Much kindness.
They seem quite content. I relish my time with them, the regularity of our meals together: the caldo we eat in the late afternoon,
their midnight chicken sandwiches, my father's ritual glass of red
wine. The gift of this child is how he has opened my eyes. I see my
mother's amazing physical beauty, the quality of her skin, still
sensual, seamless (the skin of a fifty-year-old at seventy-eight).
She dresses in front of me, stands bare breasted without shame.
Is it motherhood that has made our bodies finally shameless to
each other?*

26 agosto

*In the dream I am on the shore of the mainland. There is an island
out in the water. Tidal waves ravage it as hundreds of people rush
to the mainland for safety. The tidal waves, so huge, I am awed*

by their grandeur. The people that rush to shore are beach-goer types: white people, young, moneyed. Suddenly I realize my parents are on the island. I worry that they have been consumed by the storm. Then my father appears from out of the water. He is dressed in white. His calm is almost Christ-like as he surfaces. He walks toward the shore without fear. I wonder about my mother when suddenly she, too, appears, but her safety is threatened. There are tidal waves surrounding her. I hear a voice. It is the voice of Ellen or my sister. It tells me to go in there and save my mother. I am shocked that this has not occurred to me. I know I cannot save her, that it would be a false gesture, that I would surely drown, but the voice insists that I go in there. I awaken.

10 septiembre

I could have held him for two hours in the darkness of that nursing room, in its silence, simulating that place from where he emerged, not violently but of his own volition. But there was the fear of falling asleep while holding him bundled as he was, the fear of him falling too deeply into my arms where his breath might not find release, fear of suffocation. This is a mother's fear, I know, a mother's guilt as I bring him back into the hospital nursery. The nurse reminds me, "Probably the first time since his birth he had things so quiet."

Can I ever make it up to him, those last three months in the womb lost? Then I imagine the endless hours when he will have both silence and darkness and also the warm embrace of my breast . . . when I get him . . . when I get him home.

25 septiembre

Endless hours still yet to come in the ICN, watching our baby move from isolette to crib, from two to three to four pounds. Endless hours yet to come before I can get Rafaelito home. Two full weeks pass without crisis. Today is my birthday.

Returning from the ocean, I call the hospital, speak with Nurse Rose. She tells me Rafaelito has made me a birthday card. She tells me the story of getting his spindly legs to stay put onto the ink. His signature, a footprint in a card. Earlier today I came into the ICN, and Ellen had arranged for a cake to be awaiting me, again signed by Rafaelito. "Feliz cumpleaños, Mamá," is inscribed on top, and I still marvel at the miracle that someone will soon grow to call me Mamá.

Ellen and I walk the beach. It is all I really wanted to do for my birthday, to meditate on the glass wall of wave that crashes onto the shoreline. Sandpipers scurry along the wet sand, burrow their beaks in search of sand crabs. I remember my own child-hood. How, like the sandpipers, I learned to read the signs of where the crabs were buried, bubbles of air cracking the smooth surface of the sand, their soft-shelled bodies hidden less than an inch below.

I am too exhausted to write tonight, but I only wanted to record my bottomless joy at the entrance of Rafael into my life, of the ever-awe of what was not present with me, suddenly appearing and residing in my heart.

28 septiembre

I try to dissect the wild scrawl. Ronnie's* handwriting. He speaks of his imminent death. Although in good health, he says he considers it constantly since learning he is positive. He asks me not to write of him posthumously. "No obituaries," he says, as were done for Tede. He wants only to be remembered by his poems, as

---

* Ronnie Burk, Chicano poet, prophet, and visual artist.

we all wish, to be remembered for our poems. But I have forgotten how to write the poem, the play. I read Ronnie's letter where he mentions at least five writers I do not know, but Bob Kaufman— the Black Beat poet, now gone—was not unknown to me, and I dream of doing nothing other than reading until I know them all, until I have something to write again.

These days I feel I never fully inhabit the hours. Even while watching Rafael's small, sculpted "African head," as Myrtha calls it, while he sucks at my breast, I feel that I am missing him. I don't want to recognize the numbing frustration at the length of his hospital stay, now going into the fourth month.

30 septiembre

I don't fully absorb the recent news that there may yet be another blockage in his intestine, another cut-and-paste job on the operating table on Friday, instead of what was to have been a routine operation. I don't know the depth of my own anger until I hear myself raging on Deborah's answering machine. "There is nothing to fear but fear itself," I shout, "and it is consuming me!"

I cling to Rafaelito, hold my ears against bad news. I am that stricture, that blockage between him and all that threatens him. I grow weary of the low-level fear running concurrently with my life; that always around the corner there will be another problem the doctors failed to mention. I worry over how much intestine will be lost, over the pain Rafaelito will experience. I worry that he must go hungry for days without my milk to sustain him.

2 octubre / ICN

The second day after Rafaelito's surgery. To our relief, no more intestine was lost. "A simple procedure," the doctors had told us.

*"We'll simply reconnect the small and large intestine, and sew up
the stoma so that the baby can pass stool normally." But a day
later, it all turns out not to be so simple.*

Leaning over my son's isolette, I observe the utter exhaustion in his
frail body after the surgery. His vulnerability is almost unfathomable,
his breath shallow, broken. I glance at the monitors (a habitual instinct
by now), but to my horror, they indicate his heartbeat suddenly dropping. The dreaded cacophony of alarms follow, resounding throughout the ICN. Two nurses shove me aside. One begins to immediately
pump Rafaelito's tiny chest—an utterly delicate and insistent two-fin-
gertip compression.

No!

He stopped breathing?

Mijo? Mijito?

The alarms continue to blast off the walls of the ICN. And within
seconds, an army of rescuers converge on my baby boy, ventilator in
tow. I watch from a distance as they struggle to insert a tube down his
miniscule throat. With each jolt to his chest, I am jolted.

I can't look. I can't not look.

"Get the mother out of the room." The doctor has spotted me, as
he rushes to the scene.

And someone, gratefully, removes me. But I had already left my
body.

3 octubre / ICN

*Ellen holds Rafa in her arms. He breathes with a respirator down
into his lungs, two IVs stuck into the veins in his head, and a tube
running down his throat to suck out leakage in his stomach. He
has dehydrated, is unable to urinate. And my baby has bloated*

up to twice his body size. His face is a monster's—his eyes, black
seeds buried into a mass of fluid. When I put my hand to his
cheek to caress him, the imprint remains, deforming him.

I am more worried when the surgeon comes to see him. Dr. Azick
wears wide-ribbed corduroy pants. It is the weekend; he doesn't have
to be here, so he must be worried too. And then he admits it. "Frankly,
I'm concerned. I don't know what's wrong." I appreciate the admission, but don't like what follows: "If his condition doesn't change
soon, we'll have to go in again."

We learn later that during his pre-op preparation, the nurses,
as instructed by the surgeon, had overcleaned the intestines. I had
seen the colon cleanser going through him like Drano. The baby
was dehydrating *before* the operation, and his kidneys eventually
stopped functioning.

Ellen and I come back for a second visit that same day. After 8:00
p.m. we must enter through the emergency entrance, where a secu-
rity guard gives us passes after signing us in. The guard laboriously
tries to spell out my name, letter by letter. The pen is a stranger to
him, and I feel my impatience rise, as does my anxiety about Rafaelito. I just want to get in there and see my baby. But each night we
go through the same interrogation. "Only immediate family," the
young man tells us. He is very serious in his fresh-pressed uniform.
He is taking his job very seriously. "Yes, we know," I answer for the
hundredth time. "She (referring to Ellen) is immediate family. Call
the ICN. They'll okay us." The same old ritual, the same harassment
night after night. Then he can't help himself, and a grin begins to
crack the professional facade. "You say you're both the moms!" He
eyes his buddies, his coworkers, and the street gang begins to form
around us. Oh, they're gonna milk this one for all its worth. They are

very bored. "I didn't know two women could have a baby together."

But I am primed too. Thinking of Rafaelito swollen beyond recognition. Don't fuck with me tonight, boys. We had already filed our complaints over earlier harassment, called their supervisor who always seemed to enjoy the joke as much as they did, spoken with the ICN social worker, and in a few days, I would write the obligatory letter to the hospital administrator. Pero, para nada. Nobody really gives a damn that two women have their baby in a hospital for over three months, not knowing if he is going to live or die, and they still have to endure insults from testosterone-driven homophobes with no social power acting like they got some. My class and race analysis don't do shit for me when the brothers are standing in the way of my child. The hospital was full of AIDS patients, and Ellen and I often wondered how their lovers were treated when they came through the same door after hours.

That night I can't take any more. All I can see is Rafael's tiny face buried inside that mask of bloated flesh. "That's right," I answer, "you'd be surprised what two women can do together!" And I storm through the entrance cursing and screaming at the top of my lungs, hoping Ellen's coming up behind me. The guard is shouting after me, but I don't hear anything beyond "Hey, lady . . ." I am counting in my mind how many times we've gone through this, how many times Ellen has had to succumb to questioning when she's called the ICN and a new receptionist answers. "Who are you? What is your relationship to Rafael Moraga?" It's been over three months, for chrissakes! My impotence enrages me. I can't protect her from the pain she experiences each time they make her the outlaw. I'm the dyke in the matter, I tell myself. I'm the one who's supposed to be on the outside. But not now. As Rafael's biological mother, I am surrounded by acceptance at the hospital, until Ellen walks in and we are again the lesbian couple, the queer moms—exoticized or ostracized. I know this is new for Ellen. New and hard. As a femme, she's always passed effortlessly, that is, until she opens her mouth and the lesbian feminist spills forth without restraint.

If anyone had stopped me that night at the emergency entrance, I'm sure I would have belted him. Fortunately, no one does, and minutes later Ellen joins me at the elevator. We ride up to the third floor in silence.

4 octubre

I sit at the edge of a San Francisco fishing pier. It is minutes after dawn. This morning the fog prevents any dramatic sunrise from behind the Oakland hills, but as the ashy light gradually turns the bay waters from black to green-grey, there is renewed hope. I come to this pier today looking for hope, as I did nine months ago, having just heard the news of my pregnancy. It was a winter night, and I carried the seed of who I did not know then was Rafaelito to the pier's end. Together we floated out into the obsidian waters, harbor lights swimming inside them. We drifted under the Golden Gate and out into the Pacific sea in my dream of the future we would share. There was no doubt then (as there is less so now, learning this morning that Rafa was breathing on his own) that that future would come to pass.

A woman, middle-aged like me, interrupts this writing, asks can she take my picture. She looks familiar to me. "It's a class assignment," she says.

I respond, "I don't care." And I don't, for she has a kind smile and is a simple woman, as I am. I walk the pier in search of the simple, the daily miracles about which my son's relentless struggle to be here reminds me. The pier houses the homeless overnight. It is a stupid term for people, but that's what I call them in my mind as I pass the makeshift tents, the shopping carts pinned against royal blue plastic tarp to keep out the wind. Now a tugboat passes by, otro milagro perfectly red-and-white-striped, perfectly tugboat, steadily churning its way under the Bay Bridge. The bridge is the same color as the sky, an overcast grey. The cars travel across it, miniature in the distance, and everything becomes my baby's point of reference: the tugboat story in children's books, Tonka trucks, miniature cars that my (almost) son, Joel, used to horde and collect by the dozens.

The day has entered fully into itself now, as I hope Rafaelito will when I go to visit him this morning under the heat of warming lamps and a web of IVs. On my way back I pass joggers in sweats, thick-waisted centroamericanos in nylon windbreakers, una latina lifting her knees to her chin military-marching-style. Her morning exercises. The gulls continue to hover in anticipation of fishermen. In hours their bellies will be full of fish guts and discarded pieces of bagel. The ferries are in full steam, commuting before my eyes' horizon with ten-minute regularity.

5 octubre

The next several days are to be the last leg of this journey. Suddenly I grow afraid of how dependent we have become on the women who have nursed Rafa through these last three months: Rose, Stacey, Bobbie, Sue, Gurline, Donna, Terry, and others whom we never met who watched him throughout the night while we slept or tried to sleep.

But it is less our dependence on the nurses that concerns me, as much as the loss of the connection. These women have become our family, the only ones who have known intimately, on a daily level, the heartache we endure. I know some of them have even come to love Rafa, thinking of him as "their baby," and getting some serious attitude when he's not listed as one of theirs for the shift. Seeing them fight over Rafael tells me how attached they've become to him, and maybe, without admitting it, they've even become a little attached to us. With no "husband" in the way, Ellen and I have sat with these women till eleven on Saturday nights, shooting the shit about their love lives, their crazy jazz musician boyfriends and soon-to-be marriages in the midst of a Yugoslavian civil war. We've befriended the one dyke couple in the nursery, after it took me nearly two months to figure it out. We've talked politics, sex, fashion (at least Ellen has), and "alternative lifestyles." One time Ellen even suggested to one of the more butchy-looking nurses, who was quite a wild woman with the men, that she might want to try women for a change. Well, I guess that was going a little too far. She iced Ellen for a full month after that.

Although I am ever grateful to Dr. Azick, the soft-spoken pediatric surgeon from UCSF who saved my baby's life on that operating table, the nurses have been the real healers. We've counted on them to remember how Rafael looked the day before, to notice when his color has paled or energy waned, to respond to signals in advance when his oxygen saturation level dropped or he wasn't keeping down his food. They have advocated for him when the doctors weren't listening. They are the ones, around the clock, who have tended to my son with a woman's love, a mother's love, who have made the difference, fundamentally, in his survival.

6 octubre

In the dream, my baby has returned home to us. He is extremely vulnerable. At a theater event, I show him to my friends. He is a small worm, the color of the stoma that used to protrude from the side of his belly, a deep pinkish red. His face is a design of small markings, like brush strokes. There are no real features. I accept his appearance as perfectly normal. My friend queries, "He will grow, won't he?"

Other dreams follow the same pattern. He is so tiny, so vulnerable. I sometimes forget that I have him, start to leave a place without him. At other times Ellen forgets him. He is always on the verge of disappearing, melting away, dissolving in water.

8 octubre

Today, this day, may be the one of Rafaelito's return to us after all. It has been an everyday occurrence since Friday: the promise of his coming home, followed by the disappointment. Yet I feel the time closing in; it could surely be today. The grey dawn invites his coming. I check the date. He is a Libra baby of sorts, entering the "outside" world about ten days after his original due date. All this time he was to have been growing in my womb. Instead, he is rushed into this world and has survived a two-pound-six-ounce birth weight, two major surgeries, and myriad infections.

We have an enormous amount to be grateful for: fundamentally for his life. That he was born in 1993, not 1963, and there were surgeons to find and root out his illnesses early on. But more importantly, that from the beginning of his life he was surrounded by great love. Yes, the love from his caregivers, the nurses who came to feel Rafaelito was a part of them. But also, the love from my blood familia and all my queer relations, with candles burning across the continent toward his survival.

Throughout the wee hours of the morning, the US Air Force's
Blue Angels strip the sky of its necessary quiet. Ironic, I think,
their name, my son's name; his innocence and vulnerability
against their steel delight in stripping off the canopy of our heav-
enly protection. Angels they are not. It is too early to be awake,
and yet I know my baby will have me up at this hour most days.
I look forward to those moments of solitude with him. His crib
and cradle and changing table are covered with cloths. As if it
were Lent (I can't help thinking), awaiting the resurrection. All
is in order.

16 octubre
Rafael Angel is discharged from the hospital. More than one hun-
dred days spent in the ICN.

His release takes place a full week later than promised, always some
unexpected "complication" or "potential problem" cropping up. The
nurses keep reassuring, "It's better this way. The worse thing is to get
him home and to have to bring him back again." Unfathomable, I think.

Nurse Bobbie, fittingly, is the one to do the honors. We marvel
at how everything comes full circle, her picking Rafaelito up in Los
Angeles, admitting him in San Francisco. Now three and a half months
later, she does the paperwork for his discharge, and we load up to get
this kid home. And I mean load up: the cards, the stuffed animals,
the mobiles, the little notes Nurse Rose made in her curled calligra-
phy, the angel figures of every shade and shape, the tiny wardrobe of
T-shirts and sleepers, doll-sized knit caps and booties, the handmade
blanket from my Tía Eva, the photographs of Rafa at various stages in
his hospital stay (some with his little ICN neighbors held up by moms
and nurses grinning in the background), the thumb-sized moccasins

Cynthia and Dina brought from Pine Ridge, Deborah's healing stones and Stacey's arrowheads, the stone angel my sister gave him on her visit here, Angelina's tiny indio doll, and finally, the green-and-white-felt-covered image of la Virgen my mother had given me when I first went into the hospital over fifteen weeks earlier. I had pasted the scapular to Rafael's incubator in Hollywood on his birthday. It remained with him through the trip up north, into the operating room, and throughout his entire stay at Kaiser, San Francisco.

We pile all of this—what had decorated Rafaelito's "apartment" (the nurses' name for his crib)—onto a wheelchair, along with a bag full of medicine, complimentary diapers and formula, and a preemie-sized bathing tub (Rafa is still under five pounds). After last-minute pictures with nurses and docs, Ellen carries Rafa's car seat, I carry Rafa, and Bobbie maneuvers the wheelchair/moving van out of the ICN. As the elevator opens onto the lobby floor, Ellen and I spot two dyke moms coming in with their baby: the first and only out lesbian moms we've seen in almost four months. And this is San Francisco.

Later, stuffed into the front seat of my little truck, Ellen and I keep eyeing the sleeping bundle next to us. "Free at last." The words reverberate inside me.

*Free. At. Last.**

---

* Martin Luther King Jr., "I Have a Dream" speech, Washington, DC, 1963.

III

"YOU THE MAMA NOW."

"Babies change things,
open doors you thought were shut,
close others.
Make you into something you never been.
You the mama now,
you're gonna think different."

—Dorothy Allison
(as told to her by her mother)
Two or Three Things I Know for Sure

1

"An Uncertain Grace"

1993

Rafael Angel's first months at home were hallmarked by the ordinary and extraordinary: baby rolling over, baby sitting up, baby crawling, baby taking his first step.* Baby home for good, I prayed daily. Our lives became a series of moments that were the mundane world of sleepless nights, infant ear infections, and grown-up petty arguments. I soon saw that the susto that had taken hold of me for so long could not be so easily exorcised.

Un día de noviembre

Everything is changed. I feel something has broken in me, and yet I am forced to proceed along as if all were normal. I am a mother now, and I do not yet know how to fully inhabit that place in the world. In the small confines of my home, with Ellen, with my familia, there is a sense of rightness, but nowhere else.

---

* Due to his premature birth, Rafael's early development was quarterly monitored through home visits by an infant development specialist. Happily, he always stayed on "schedule."

Those last weeks in the hospital, we waited each day to see that Rafaelito was assimilating his food properly. There had been diarrhea, blood in the stool. We waited. Now I wonder how long to wait for a cry to stop or what his cries mean. I am awake before and through the dawn while the rest of the house sleeps. There is a restlessness in me, not due to lack of sleep, but lack of confidence. My writer's heart feels stolen by the struggle for my baby's survival. I miss the immersion into my writing terribly, fear I will not be able to resurrect that impassioned momentum. My work and its requirements return: the teaching jobs, speaking gigs, the play commissions. But there is no sustained writing time. Such moments become fugitive intervals in a twenty-four-hour clock of maintenance.

The baby cries. Sleep deprivation. I remember my comadres warning me of this physical state, near-madness. Rafael was used to round-the-clock daylight in the Intensive Care Nursery. Darkness does not mean sleep to him. He awakens three or four times a night. One night at 2:30 a.m. I break down, move out of the bed with Ellen and into Rafael Angel's room. I throw the futon on the floor, cover it with flannel sheets and the down comforter, stick the kid inside, and we sleep like odd-sized twins together. I throw him the tit at his every stirring, and he falls out again. Adding up the hours this way, I get more sleep than waiting for his squeal from the next room, feeding him, then coaxing him back to sleep for two hours. Ellen definitely gets more sleep. I worry, what does this mean? The child has moved my woman and me into separate beds. But I assure myself it is a temporary arrangement.

Oh, there are those moments of peace. Getting in the bath with Rafa, I see his body relax in a way I imagine it hasn't since utero.

Floating floating. His fists unclench, his arms fall back to the sides of his head, his chest receives the water. Yes, a baby seal, his sweet slick skin, that sense of belonging. I almost detect a smile.

According to the book, Rafaelito should be smiling by now, by his "adjusted age."* Still, there is no clearly convinced smile, only an impressive, intelligent frown.

I hate baby books. I only turn to them to make sure I am making no grave errors. I resent these white male pediatrician-types with their nurse-wives and seven kids "bonding" their way into my Mexican psyche. Rafael was born with a seriousness about him. It was the place of strength he drew from to fight the diseases that plagued him at birth. His smiles will come.

8 diciembre

I sneak out my journal for twenty minutes of writing (if I'm lucky) before Rafaelito rises with his morning cry. Some days are more difficult than others. Some days Rafael Angel is a nonstop complaint from seven in the morning till midnight. Ellen refutes it, but I know it is when we start the day arguing. About time schedules. About time. I know he senses something "off." Even though I hold him as I cry and repeat over and over again, "Esto no tiene nada que ver contigo, hijo," I can't rid myself of the knowledge of how young I was when I felt my mother's unhappiness. "At her breast," a psychic once told me, and her words come as no surprise.

Ellen spent an hour with me today (an hour she didn't have) trying to encourage me to continue with my work. At the lowest point in my physical stamina, I fall into a deep funk about my writing; it hovers hopelessly neglected. Ellen's own work life is

---

* A premature baby's adjusted age is determined by their due date (or the date on which they actually leave the hospital) rather than the premature birthdate.

burdened with programming and budget deadlines, community meetings and the stress of maintaining a theater and a public political face. But she thrives on the challenge of it all.

The baby cries. Again.

I want to smother a slowly surfacing guilt that my concern has shifted from baby to work too quickly. Less than two months ago, I worried for his life. I still worry, only the anxiety has abated somewhat. And in the lessening of the fear, there is a small aperture, a glimmer of a longing to create again. Oh, it's a luxury to be sure, reserved for the well-fed and healthy (when Rafa's life was threatened, I couldn't write a line); but now, coming out from under the sea of that susto, I need the work, the writing, more passionately than ever. I need to know I am more than these tasks of motherhood, more than mother. I need to remember that I am a writer.

12 diciembre / Día de Guadalupe

This is my first visit with my son to the Sacred Tree in Watsonville. I have come with Ricardo and our friend Ricky to fulfill la promesa y dar gracias a la Virgen de los Cannery Workers for saving my baby's life. I especially have a need to ask for counsel. There has been a relentless rigidity in me since the baby's birth, more so since his return home. I maintain a furious order in the house, and Ellen often complains of it, feeling a stranger in her own home.*

Rafaelito is so tiny I can wrap him up in my rebozo and nurse him unnoticed under the shelter of the oaks. I nurse and rock, nurse and rock, as the women sing oraciones a la Virgen in

---

* In 1992, the image of la Virgen de Guadalupe was spotted on an old oak tree in the Mexican-California town of Watsonville, an hour down the coast from San Francisco. Peregrinos (pilgrims) continue to visit the site with supplications.

that flat Mexican key de las viejitas. Ricardo and Ricky stand in the outer circle of prayer. There, all the men are gathered, vaquero hats in their hands; their black hair glistens in the sunlight.

It is difficult to see through the crowd of women surrounding the tree, but I spot the head of a woman (a mother) bent over her child who has been brought before la Virgen's image. The child is about six or seven, sitting in a tall stroller. I had noticed him as we first arrived, his long legs hanging down from the high seat. (Too old for a stroller, I think.) I didn't realize he was unable to walk until now as the mother pulls the boy up, grabbing him under the arms. A small group of mujeres encircle him. La jefa, a woman in her seventies, a thick rope of grey braid going down her back, holds her hands over the boy's head, asking for la Virgen's intercession. "Ayúdale que camine este pobrecito niño" is the prayer. Help the boy walk.

The mother and the other women pull the child around on spaghetti legs. He's loving it, being the center of attention, bobbing about in front of the crowd. He wears a sweet payaso grin on his face. I wish to God the kid would get up and walk, too, but hate seeing them put him through it. The hope. Maybe he is too young to hope like we do. Maybe he is just having a good time. But the mother isn't. Crying up a storm when the boy doesn't walk, probably knowing he isn't going to. Hoping against hope. And I am there in that mother's skin, as I pull Rafaelito into me, holding on for his dear life, his dear health. Knowing I could've been her. Still can.

Sometimes I fear what would happen should Rafael ever get seriously ill again. My memory of his near-death is so close to me, still so visceral in my own gut. At times, when Rafaelito exhibits even the slightest sign of a cold, I feel that sudden rush of adrenaline, that panic. I fear he will not survive. I know the fear is not logical, that it emerges from that region where I carry the memory of his two-pound spirit being rolled down the hospital corridor on his way to surgery. Those same deep dark eyes looking up at me as if to reassure me he would indeed survive. I am afraid of loving this much, afraid to be so vulnerable to the fragile life of another human being.

Take my life instead, I can say without hesitation.

Later that night, I sit at the side of my baby's cradle and gradually rock him to sleep. It is always something of a miracle that I can coax him to sleep without trickery, just putting him down, well-fed, he drifting off into slumber. I watch the slow rise and fall of his chest. There is always a subtle rocking to his body as he sleeps, the same rocking I remember we discovered in the ICN. Each time Rafaelito was released from the cradle of our arms and returned to his isolette, he would continue the movement, the ritmo, the motion of comfort, of cariño, of continuance.

Days later...

In honor of la Virgen's feast day, Ricardo had given Rafaelito his first "picture book." (That's what Ricardo called it.) An Uncertain Grace, photographs by Brazilian Sebastião Salgado. I am struck by an image I spy over Ellen's shoulder as she flips the pages. An African woman supports the bodies of two starving babies as they each suck from her breasts. The breasts sag, aged and milkless into their mouths.

At first all I see es el horror de la hambre. Then I look more deeply and notice the delicate vein running along the woman's arm, the grace and beauty of those babies' proud chests, muscu-

*lar limbs, the strength and desire for life in those fists that grab at
the woman's breasts. The twins are my son, his pathetic thinness
at birth, his clinging animal heart and hunger.*

*The woman remains faceless in the photograph, but I know
how she looks. I know her infinite fatigue, the futility of a suck
that can draw no sweet succor, no sustenance. She feels herself
an empty woman. Her breasts, brown barren sacks of crumpled
paper, such thirsty breasts. One baby, with the fine hard African
skull, wears a beaded necklace. Against all odds for his survival,
this baby's entrance into the world is decorated. These twins are
my baby's cousins. Like him, they are survivors.*

*In an inscription in the book, Ricardo wrote to Rafael: "Para
su primer día de Lupita, que nuestra belleza, lucha y cultura siem-
pre te llene." There was a rush of emotion reading the words, a resonance, an echo I felt, a longing met. Those are the words that keep
me from saying so freely to Ellen, "Yes, should I pass on, the baby
goes to you alone, unequivocally." Es la cuestión de la cultura.*

*There is no denying that I had this baby that he might be a
Mexican, for him to know and learn what it means for him to
hold that inheritance in his body, to feel el fuego, la riqueza, la
llamada de lo mexicano. And for a moment, I miss that Mexican
loving in my life. I know this is the "half-breed" in me speaking;
she who stands at the generational crossroad of a family. She who
bears witness to the Mexican vanishing without protest into the
generation that succeeds her. She who wants to not vanish as a
person. As a pueblo.*

Sueño

*I dream that Cathy and I are being instructed in Aztec danza
by a Xicana, una maestra. In conversation with one of the male*

leaders (a sloppily dressed macho), La Maestra complains that there are no babies present. In order to appease her, the man brings her another woman's child. She is not pleased. She is worried that it is separated from its mother.

We dance in a circle. La Maestra gives Cathy a unique kind of tambor with two bowl-like parts; one part has a kind of paddle with which to drum. I am only given the one piece without the paddle. I am disappointed because I want to learn to play the tambor.

But as we dance, she begins to instruct me—half-piece that I am.

El Día de Nochebuena / San Gabriel

Only before dawn can I find the silence and the solitude to write, here in the home of my youth. It is strangely ironic that my baby of nearly six months sleeps peacefully in the bedroom that once enclosed my anguished adolescent dreams of desire. The same desire called him into being onto this planet and now roots him here among the family of his maternal grandmother's namesake: Moraga.

Coming home will never be the same, coming home with this child. I will now always return a mother. Mother: the term assumes the shape of my being very gradually.

Yesterday I heard the word fall from my sister's mouth as she plays with Rafaelito. I was, for a moment, taken aback when I realized that she was not referring to our mother but speaking to my son of me. We laughed at my still-virgin response. The intellect not quite caught up to biology.

It is now early morning, and my baby swings idly in an electric contraption meant just for such purposes. My mother warms the tortillas on the comal and my dad finishes off breakfast. Rafael is

content, lulled by the steady rhythm of the automatic swing and
still within watchful eye of his ever-growing familia. My mother
sighs, "Ay, they grow up so fast."

I know exactly what she means; this baby swinging in the
doorway is already somewhere in time a very old man, and I and
my parents are long gone. There is a way that Rafael's arrival
is an announcement of their own imminent passing. My parents
wonder, I know, how much of his growing up they will be privileged to witness. "In good health," my mother adds. I wonder the
same. At times like these, I want to hold on desperately to the
moment. We record history as it passes from holiday to holiday,
visit to visit, with a kind of tacit agreement that the photos and
cards—the documentation—may have to suffice for my son as
the reflection of an enormous familial love he may not consciously
remember by the time he is fully grown.

Days ago, we visited the gravesite of my abuelita in East LA.
My Tío Bobby, Tía Eva, and my parents encircled the tomb-
stone. I wondered, as I placed my son onto the rug of crew-cut
lawn blanketing the spot, if these two did not already know
each other. Could Rafael be the messenger boy of the now-dead
matriarch?

My tío speaks to his mother con puro cariño. "Mi querida
Mamá, mi preciosa," he intones, as my mother and tía pick at
the crabgrass scratching the edges of the gravestone. We fill a tin
can with water, put a handful of garden roses from my mother's
garden into it and into the mouth of the grave. We place a holiday poinsettia next to it. We pray the rosary como si fuera un
canto, my mother leading the song. This is how my family honors
its dead.

In the months ahead, I will learn of Myrtha's father's passing. It is not such sad news: a ninety-four-year-old man joins his wife, barely a year after her passing. The good news is that Myrtha had brought him home from the hospital; her son took his abuelo into his arms, bathed him, held him like a baby, and rocked him unto death. Don Rafael's final wish: to go from home to grave in Arecibo, Puerto Rico. And so it was.

I light a veladora for him and find the medal of San Rafael that Nurse Rose had given me. I hang it over the head of the flame.

"What did the old man die of?" I ask Myrtha's friend who had first relayed the news.

"An obstruction in the intestine," she responds. "There was blockage where the small and large intestine meet." Her words chill me. "It's very serious."

"Yes," I answer. "I know." And I wonder at the meaning of the news, that Don Rafael should die of the exact same condition that Rafaelito had suffered at birth, that I had named my son Rafael, never consciously knowing Myrtha's father's name nor that her brother who had died in childhood carried the same. Spirits become flesh, then give up the ghost of the body only to become flesh, again. Or so I have come to believe; there is meaning in this web we weave of human relations.

31 diciembre / Back in San Francisco

Since Rafaelito's entrance into this life with us, exhaustion domi-
nates all other feelings. Still, Ellen and I wait up anyway to greet
the new year in the steely cold of this December San Francisco night.
    Ellen reads.
    Rafael sleeps.
    I write.

I write to remind myself on the eve of the new year that I am a writer, although I return from my ten-day stay in LA not quite convinced. I see Spielberg's new movie of the Jewish Holocaust and I am reminded of the human capacity for the most brutal and obscene cruelties. I question what I am worth, never having confronted that life-and-death choice between honor and survival. To sacrifice oneself for others is the most noble, the most human response; survival instinct, the most banal. For what is survival other than animal?

I am an animal for my child. I knew that watching the mothers in the film, separated from their children, clawing at their enemy like wild, wounded lionesses. I am too exhausted to write more. I only want to ask—what am I doing about man's capacity for cruelty?

On that I end the year.

2

Metamorphosis

1994[*]

They say that snakes go blind for a while
before they shed their skin for the last time.

—Toni Morrison, *Jazz*

May Day

"*There is nothing left over,*" *I tell her.*

Is it blind rage that spills out from me on the edge of despair, of transformation? Am I blind to love, to the real heartache reflected in Ellen's eyes? I think of nothing but myself, my son.

I remember the astrologer assuring me. "Forty-two," *she said,* "will mark the end of the seven-year cycle. A breakthrough of the old pattern," *she predicted.* "You will have resolved your relationships to such a degree that they will no longer serve as obstacles to your writing."

---

[*] Journal entries become fewer and further between as I return to my teaching and writing schedule, and to the growing requirements of a growing infant.

But I feel no such resolve. Not today.

This much I know: I will never write the same. Maybe that is part of the metamorphosis the astrologer predicted. With the appearance of Rafael in my life, I can never return to the writer I once was. Not because of the time constraints, which are considerable, but because my soul is never completely empty in the same way. I am conscious of another entity always pulling on me. I don't know really how the Medea play emerged, even in the rough form the work presently wears, but the writing did not feel the same. Ironically, it did not take a piece of me in the same way earlier writing has. It is no less challenging, but now an aperture has been created through which my child passed, and the art seems to move through that same opening. I can't say how, exactly, only that there is a permeability in the process that wasn't there before.

I am trying to be a mother who writes well. I am trying to be a writer who mothers well. Somewhere inside me, an opposing force rises up to stop one or the other. Perhaps it is the measure of that very aperture that leaves me awestruck by the breadth and depth of its promise or (more sobering) of its requirements.

Rafaelito watches me write. He is no longer interested in the baby gym set dangling in the corner. He is interested in the movement of my hand across this page. Black strokes against the soft beige grain of this paper. He watches me. And for the first time it occurs to me that he may have something to learn from me, by my example.

"This is my work, hijo. I am a writer."

Con el paso del tiempo ...

I try to teach Rafael Angel hide & seek. I throw a cloth over a small blue plastic block. He realizes it has vanished. It appears that he understands, for the first time, that the block may be underneath the cloth, if he were to take a look. But those are too many ifs to bother with right now. I can see him thinking this, as his almond eyes roll over, ever so subtly, to another toy clearly visible and attainable. He goes for it, springing onto it like a young cub. And I begin to laugh, the deepest laugh, the richest of familial laughs. I bring Rafa into my arms, and every cell of my body is filled with joy at his entrance into this world, his developing and discriminating mind, his pure presence. I laugh so hard I cry, and wet his face with my tears, my kisses, my hope, recalling the nearness of his almost death.

The advent of solstice ...

Last night I laid on one end of the couch, listening to the arias of Maria Callas, Rafaelito asleep in my arms. Ellen was stretched out on the other end, hand on my foot. I thought about what it is to create, even for a single moment, a thing of beauty, a thing of pure and honest human passion, as these arias. I thought of my own task as a writer—a life task to write anything that comes close, even for a moment, to the depth of human emotion. At times I question it all. I wondered if I can ever truly create a complete work, something I can stand in the center of and know its wholeness.

Metamorphosis. Change. Transformación.

Tonight es una noche triste. After a typically fog-covered San Francisco morning and a beautiful summerlike afternoon, this evening in this silent room seems sad. Is change sad? A letting go? I am afraid to look at how fundamentally Rafa's presence *in our lives has changed Ellen and me—each, her own life, and our life together. There is no return. Is it the past, singular "I" that I mourn, that freedom? I scarcely remember her and wonder about this new me. This writer-mother. This often-troubled lover. The sage smoke brings a kind of calm, the smell comforting, cleansing. There is the need for quiet, like the breath between arias, reading into the late evening with Ellen nearby, the baby resting peacefully.*

3 julio
Rafael's first birthday / New York City

Ironically, I repeat the very journey I took last year, six months pregnant, feet and hands swelling in steaming subway stations, walking down 42nd Street each day toward the Hudson on my way to rehearsal, then finally joining Ellen at the Cape to recover.

Now, I have returned to New York to see The Heart of the Earth *through its final phase of rehearsals for the world premiere. Rafa's "Tía Cathy" has come with me to care for Rafaelito while I work at the theater. Since his coming home, Cathy's care and love for Rafa have emerged so spontaneously and with such heart that I've come to count on her daily. She is familia for us, with no strings attached, just our enduring friendship and Rafa's reciprocated soul connection, as the ties that bind.*

Today is his birthday, and as it is the Fourth of July weekend, we have the day off to celebrate. We stuff Rafaelito into the stroller and make our way to Central Park, stopping here and there for party supplies: an ice chest of beer, a carrot cake, a loaf of French bread, cheese, a candle in the shape of the number one. Ricardo and posse meet us in front of the Museum of Natural

History across from the park. *This brown queerboy contingent has been in New York for weeks now to celebrate the twenty-fifth anniversary of Stonewall. But they know they are not fully a part of those festivities, although it was their kind that started the rebellion a quarter of a century ago. They are not white nor monied nor just gay; they are "coloredqueerboys." And in that sense, how glad I am to be in their company, to bring my son into their circle of fine and critical minds, smart mouths, and indignant dignity.*

We party.

Ricardo holds Rafaelito while Cathy tries to get him to blow out his candle. I snap the camera. To capture the time, to remember this picture of youth: elegant dark limbs stretched across the damp summer-green grass, their laughter. I felt that way once too, when New York was thoroughly contained in my lesbian-coloredgirl grasp. Rafael fidgets in Ricardo's arms. We blow the candle out for him, and I make a wish like a prayer that my son will always have such men, such hope, in his life.

4 julio

Maybe it is the motionless humidity of this city, maybe the sheer fact of the anniversary, that causes me to remember Rafaelito's sudden birth in a way I had never before. Something brings me back to that moment in time. San Gabriel. Hitting the bed just after breakfast, the water breaking open inside of me, and I feared my tiny baby had broken open, too. But he waited. Warrior that he is, he waited, and on the seventh day he came, on the seventh day of labor rooms, heart monitors, IVs, fear of infection. As I ly flat on my back and praying, my baby entered this world. Born in Los Angeles, as the generation before him.

*What is hardest to write about is the loss I feel not hav-
ing brought Rafael to full term. At times I think it is loss, then
wonder if it's really guilt I feel, that my son had to go through
so much suffering outside the womb because I couldn't protect
him inside. There's no one to blame really, no matter how many
times I run all the events through my mind:*

- *I am standing on a subway train, my feet so swollen. And a
  young woman offers me her seat. In all my years of subway
  riding in New York City, no one had ever offered me a seat.
  I don't understand why the woman keeps gesturing to the
  seat she has just vacated for me, until I realize that she can
  see I am pregnant. I gracefully decline, determined as I am
  to balance my weight with the jostling of the train. I figure
  the baby finds the movement comforting como una cuna
  rocking. But maybe I should have accepted her offer . . .*

- *As I should have refused a week later to walk any further,
  just sat myself down on the Cape Cod sand until they found
  me. Instead, I walked, trying in vain to look for Ellen's aging
  mother. Then, too, losing sight of Ellen as she headed across
  the sand dunes I walked . . .*

- *As I had on that Southern California beach with my shat-
  tered brother-in-law and through that labyrinth of shopping malls with my ever-eager sister.*

- *Maybe it was vanity that got in the way of thinking sensibly
  about my health. Six months pregnant and I never felt more
  beautiful, more "in shape," the round in my belly making me
  feel more woman, more wholly female. It was a new feeling
  that drew me.*

- *I walked and walked to keep up that healthy rounding
  shape. Good for both of us, I told myself. And . . .*

- *Soon, I would return home, stick my feet up on a lawn chair, and do nothing all San Francisco summer long but devote myself full time to the task of growing larger with life.*
- *I had scheduled my work accordingly.*
- *I had canceled all travel by the seventh month (as recommended by my nurse)*
- *But the seventh month never came.*

Beyond these ruminations and self-recriminations, I feel something deeper. I see pregnant women into their seventh and eighth and ninth month and envy them. I measure the shape of their bellies against what I remember of my own. Did I get that far with my baby? How big was I? I don't experience this in a covetous way. I only long to recuperate those last three months of communion, getting big and fat and full of Rafa.

Sometimes I just chalk it up to one phrase: he was in a hurry to get here. I daily witness that quality in Rafaelito, always ahead of himself, always frustrated that his body hasn't quite caught up to where his spirited intelligence wants to take him.

I take hold of my breast, slide my fingers down to the nipple, squeeze the tip between my thumb and forefinger. This is how to get the milk going. To my surprise, a thick, rich yellow liquid spills out. I try the other side. Same thing. Although I go through this ritual every few months or so, checking to see if I can still make milk, this time, after days and days of writing, days and days of remembering those last weeks of pregnancy, the liquid is as thick as the day I gave birth. I think, I could start all over again.*

---

* I nursed Rafaelito for nearly a year until his gut began to show some disturbance and he was gradually weaned onto a formula recommended by his

I do miss it, at times, that intimacy with Rafael, remembering those tiny fingers greedily clamoring for my breast in the dark, finding it and latching on. His mouth, a kiss that lasted. At those moments, I felt I could recover a bit of the loss for both of us, our sudden separation from each other. And possibly that, too, is what this writing serves: to recover the loss by reliving those moments of first motherhood.

I stop here, put down my pen, cross to my son sleeping face down on the bed. I take him into my arms and marvel at his good health, his sturdy "thunder thighs," and the rich copper-rose color of his face. I just feel so damn grateful, as I am for Ellen, remembering her Amazon strength, her Irish outrage, her basic loyalty during the hardest year of my life.

Mid-July / Cape Cod

After New York, we return to this house at the Cape, Rafa now full bloom in my arms. We have settled into our stay here with an open ease, and I feel myself very present with Ellen, awed by her beauty. We touch each other. Often. There is a newness to the feeling, although it is always difficult mustering (not the word), conjuring (not the word), getting some full sex here. The house is quite small, and for what might've sounded like a fancy address, its thin walls harbor few secrets.

It is very early morning, and the choice is between sleep and awakening to find these few moments alone to read and write. Rafael sleeps balled up into the corner of the port-a-crib, Ellen lies belly-up, her hands cradling her pelvis that had her up earlier with menstrual cramps. In the next room, Ellen's mother lies in a diagonal fetal position across her bed. Through the always-

---

pediatrician.

open crack of her door, I can see the well-shaped aging feet resting
one upon the other. She's had another sleepless night, I ascertain
from the reading glasses and curled paperback abandoned on
the kitchen table, the open pack of solitaire cards next to them.
I wonder how her mood will be today. All is dependent on the
quality of her night's rest. When her body turns enemy—refusing
sleep, spasming senselessly, stiffening in every joint—she becomes
distant, preoccupied. But last night all those pains had vanished,
and she was pure delight. She, Ellen, and I sat together well past
midnight, drinking margaritas and telling stories. She was in her
old best form, a spirited hard-hittin' talker, like her daughter.

The house rattles. Ellen's mom must be up. I am beginning
to recognize the sounds of her movements. During the first two
nights here, the small, staggered steps confused me. I thought
them Rafael's, and I would awaken with a start. Ellen doesn't
awaken, accustomed to the movements of her mother, who crip-
ples steadily. "Cripple." I cringe at the harshness of the word. But
what language is there to describe that physical betrayal by the
body in old age? Hers, more marked because of the Parkinson's,
yet I observe it in my own parents, less dramatically, but nonethe-
less sudden. Always too sudden. I witness my friends and their
friends die overnight in their thirties and forties.* I remember
my comadres who have always gone without. Without mothers,
while mothers themselves. And I realize the blessings of longevity
and good health among my blood relations.

Paul Monette's lover of ten years is dying. His book open on
my lap, I nod off to sleep. I dream I am dying of AIDS. We are
all dying.

---

* By 1995 AIDS deaths in the US would reach an all-time high.

Provincetown on the Cape

We spend the night at an inn. At 5:50 a.m. I give the baby a bottle and struggle to get him to sleep again. An hour later I am wide awake, and he is warming my spot in the bed next to Ellen, sound asleep. I grab my journal and hit the streets. I love the opening up of a day, sitting on a park bench in front of the P-town city hall. Twenty minutes ago, before I found this cup of coffee, the only noticeable activity was the middle-aged joggers, the recycling truck, and the shopkeepers sweeping up the brick sidewalks in front of their stores after a night's queer frolicking. It is a comfort, even as white as P-town is, to be able to walk these streets unafraid with the baby on my back and Ellen in hand. It is a comfort after the queer wasteland of the rest of the Cape.

P-town is a gay resort, although in the ten years or more since my first visit, it is glaringly evident that this place has suffered the loss of thousands of gay men. I can't really imagine the number who have visited here, now gone. AIDS virtually decimated Fire Island's gay life. They say the Provincetown Chamber of Commerce is beginning to worry cuz the dykes aren't nearly enough (in numbers or money) to sustain this resort town. So P-town is being pumped to the hets as a great place to bring the kids. And they do show up, little nuke families of 2.5 children, with daddy, always a hopelessly closeted queen, in the lead. By 9:00 p.m., however, they've all disappeared to their hotel cable TVs, and P-town once again plays gracious hostess to its ever-faithful queer clientele.

I could stay here forever in this mode—reading and writing. Since I left San Francisco at the end of June, I have gone through such a range of emotions. One is the admission that I miss my morning writing time. Mornings were always my most creative hours, rolling out of a dream onto a page. A few days ago on the beach, I had been trying to finish the same page of Monette's memoir for fifteen minutes but kept getting interrupted by Rafa's insistent whine. I gave up. I stuffed Rafaelito into the carrying pack and onto my shoulders, announcing that "I have no internal life," and stormed down the beach. High drama. I left Ellen with that comment, wanting to hurt her with it a little, wanting to blame someone.

Ellen complains of how slowly I move lately. It took me all morning to pack up the kid and me yesterday leaving for Provincetown. But I can't move any more quickly than that. Slowing down, I feel a deep weariness come to the surface of my bones, my skin. It is a residual exhaustion, the culmination of a full year and a half of endless work and worry: becoming pregnant, carrying Rafa for twenty-eight weeks, the three and a half months Rafael spent in the ICN, the first year of his life adjusting to being here, our adjusting to him. The sleepless nights, the colds, his bowel problems, the writing deadlines in the midst of baby care, the relationship struggles because of baby care.

These days I am aware of a nameless ache inside of me. A longing for contemplation, reflection, solitude. I respond to it only in long walks along the beach, Rafaelito on my back. His excited kicks dig into my hips until he is lulled by the rhythmic rocking of my slow stride along the shore. The kicks subside; he sleeps. And I move into a kind of walking meditation.

The water here reflects the color of what I have only seen in the Mexican Caribbean. But this is not a Mexican sea; it is New England. In the distance I see Ellen emerge from it, emerald seagreen. This is her color. The green of her eyes, her nature. This is her home, her immigrant land. I consider the two land masses of our origins—Northeast and Southwest—and wonder how she *and I ever found each other, starting from such opposite edges of the continent.*

Ellen and I drift a distance from each other. Still, there is a thin, sure cord between us. We keep the other afloat in a sea of an unspoken silence, so many dreams private and singularly sown.

Do we drift apart?

Her mother pulls her to the land of her childhood, and what of mine ... ?

Still, as the sun begins to disappear into the horizon, I think I could grow to love this place, begin to attach the smells and the texture and the wet weight of the night air to a sustained memory, and make this strange land of occupying gringos something of my own. I watch my son take his own small-fisted hold of it.

Soon, should we continue to return each year, he will begin to remember Nana's home. Remember the nightly walk to the neighborhood pond. Remember the four ducks in perfect symmetrical harmony swimming in the pool of a full moon's reflection.

"Mira la luna," I said, days ago, pointing to the moon's uncompromised fullness. Will he remember "luna"? She, too, seems a kind of stranger here, a bit foreign in this land of sudden summer storms and fierce bright winters.

She is a Mexican moon.

And I dream of a desert in which to bury us all one day.

Mother, lover, child.

All.

3

La Sonámbula

1995

*M*onths have passed in what I remember as the haze of *a prolonged and private illness,* an acute exhaustion, a longing for respite, finding none.

I feel I haven't really slept since the baby was born. How afraid I am—it feels so profound—to lay my head upon the pillow, that I may not rise up again. I want to escape into a very deep sleep. All is my baby these days, and little remains for the rest of me... us...

What is this relentless exhaustion? The sudden rise in my body temperature, these cold sweats? I call and cancel all speaking engagements. I feel foolish that I know so little of myself, my limitations. How deep my weariness runs; quick Band-Aid fixes are not sufficient. How do I make a living? How do I give my child, my partner, the love they need? I worry about my "irregular" lifestyle—not my lesbianism, but my art; how it makes me travel out of town, work nights, depend on the generosity of family and friends for childcare. I plot it all out compulsively weeks in

95

advance. *It is never enough.*

I feel I have been asleep for days, endless days. I attribute it to jetlag, but I return home from a week's work of travel and I am still sleep-walking. I am someplace, not here.

I spy Rafael's smiles, his open-heartedness, his full presence that mirrors the hollowness of my absence. I feel guilty that I am missing Rafa, always missing him when my heart is pulled else-where inside myself. His wakefulness shames me in comparison. I fear my obsessions. I fear anything that draws me away from this growing up of my child, but when I do not attend to my heart, I walk about asleep anyway, como una sonámbula.

I see an anger developing in Rafaelito. He threw a tantrum this morning not knowing if he wanted his shoes on or off. I watch him in this stage of life before full words, before I realize that exactly what he needs is to sleep like me. He, too, is exhausted, fighting cold after cold, ear infection after ear infection. I worry about all these health problems. Worry we're getting these viruses now from places where the environment has been ravaged and the earth's venganza returns to us the size of microbes. Is this paranoia or common sense?

Rafael awakens mid-sleep and utters a pained cry. I pat him softly and he drifts off again. Is it just that he needs to know we are there, or does he remember awakening at 3:00 a.m. under the hot glare of hospital lamps, no mama in sight, a sharp pain piercing his gut? I wonder where in his small body he has put all that suffering and what traces of it will reside in him as a grown man. An old man.

Santa Monica
This Southern California oceanside hotel offers some respite with

its trestles of bougainvillea, its terra cotta–tiled patio, its intended suggestion of a Mexican paradisal holiday. I sleep endlessly. (Rafa is staying with my mother.) I cannot get enough sleep to restore those places in me virtually drained of all vitality.

I sit by the hotel pool with Ellen. The world is brighter today, although the sea-sky threatens to break into thick rain; although my heart feels thick with breaking. Ellen dreams of a Hollywood lifestyle; the locality, no doubt, has inspired it. For my part, I have no cinematic landscapes in my mind, only the lingering memory of the images that arrested me this morning.

I woke up thirsty, having slept all night with a stuffed nose and open mouth. In the dream, the hotel's jardinero wants to know why the gringos bring so much water with them. He means the rains, but I explain their fear of drinking Mexican water. Then the dream shifts to birds, hovering overhead, that look identical to babies but are really flying monsters. They have an insatiable hunger. Is it all me—this thirst, this hunger, the threat of what I perceive as my baby's ravenous animal need?

Easter Sunday / San Gabriel

I kneel in the yellowing wooden pew of my childhood church. Mass is being celebrated in honor of the parish's new converts. My father is one of them, draped in the same confirmation gowns I wore at twelve. My Tío Bobby, as his sponsor, stands behind him on the altar steps. I watch the back of my father's balding head, that pink spot amid the last few feathers of a silver crown. Somehow in it I sense my father's vulnerability. He is receiving God. I know this is what he is thinking. After nearly five decades of living among us Mexican Catholics, my father has become one of "us." But I know I am no longer one of "them."

A two-and-a-half-hour service, and I am left spent and resentful. An empty ritual. I do not say this for the others, for my father's newfound faith. I say it for myself and my son, until he can speak for himself. My Catholicism—its Mexican symbols, its Indianism—is such a private prayer to me that it no longer even resembles the religion. I am a heretic, not because I am faithless but because I am a believer of something else that cannot reside here beneath these midcentury wooden rafters.

What to teach Rafael?

I know this much: that there is the small spirit-place we occupy in the universe, in the collective soul; that a lighted candle can ignite the fire of hope, of faith, of shared prayer; that shared prayers can stop wars, cure wounds, mend hearts. I believe this. I believe in an emptiness that can be filled with selflessness. I don't know how to arrive there. I don't know how to even find the path, but I will clamber toward it in the dark with my son by my hand. Until it is time to let go.

A year ago, I relinquished Rafaelito to his godparents at the baptismal fount of a humble East Los Angeles church. It is the church of the poor, and the presiding priest, a pastor of the poor, pilgrimaged with Cesar Chavez on the long walks of protest for the UFW.* This credential suited me fine because the baptism I sought for my son had nothing really to do with the Catholic Church and everything to do with the home culture of faith that had raised me. The baptism was to be my son's public initiation into the community of his familia, with all my blood relations in attendance. And they all, beautifully, did show up. Still, when los padrinos returned Rafaelito's newly christened body back into my arms, I felt I had betrayed

---

* United Farm Workers

him. I held him tight against the breast of an unanswered prayer. I wanted to protect my son from deceit, from the failure of male gods and god-fearing males.

That night I dreamt murder, mayhem. I dream: them against us.

Ellen and I are going to slaughter. Along with dozens of women, we are to be executed en masse. There is a war going on, and we have been taken captive. I realize I have been separated from Rafael and that he is alone in our apartment. I shout this out loud, hoping I will be spared to save my son. This is exactly what happens. A guard hears me and takes pity. He leaves a gate open through which I can escape. Of course, Ellen (not being the "real" mother) is not allowed out, but to my great relief I learn that she, too, is released later.

I have constructed my daily life, to the degree possible, outside the prison of patriarchy. This is not a rhetorical statement. I protect/protest my life by separateness, by secrets, by never speaking aloud my own spiritual creed. This is the fact of my existence and the home-world in which I will raise my son. I am not fooled. *They* are not fooled. Even motherhood does not make me loyal to *them*.

Here in Southern California where it snows in the foothills during Easter week, birds of paradise grow to the size of monsters and their urgent beak-mouths gape open to the heavens. Are they hungry too? For what? The foreboding rains? It is springtime and Easter and I try to convince my aching bones, my ailing heart, that the season will bring a change, a resurrection of hope, a return of faith—in what? I hold the gift of this child, and still I feel without resolve.

I dream I have lost everything. All material possessions. I have lost my writing on the most profound of levels. No trace of it is left. It is as if all that I had previously written has disappeared.

I am hysterical. Like a child, I wail on the floor. I throw a fit. Ellen is a man in the dream. S/he is having a business meeting with an artist. S/he is no comfort, s/he cannot console me. I go to my room, continue my ranting and raving. Myrtha enters. I tell her what has happened. "Moving out of the darkness into the light." This is the phrase that comes to me. She tells me this is all a blessing: to begin again as an artist, completely clean, from scratch, relieved of the burden of the past, of your previous writings.

Returning home, I awaken with the weight of a small stone upon my chest. I feel Ellen's name etched into the stone. Is it her, or only a nameless uncertainty in me? We go about our lives in separate orbits. I want the distance.

I must confess that in some of my imaginings of the future, I do not see her clearly formed there. I only know my son's constant presence. He is familia. Maybe "lover" has been replaced with "mother," but it does not satiate. At times, I miss the sex, fear how remote it has become between Ellen and me. Worse, I fear it no longer matters to me, which I know is a lie, a camouflaged sentiment waiting in the bushes to jump out and fall upon some other woman's bones.

It's so hard with Ellen—her ceaseless energy, her ambition and drive—what I had once so admired in her now seems to invade my life. I blame her, unfairly, for the muffled voice inside me that I cannot decipher: it is my writer's voice. My home has become my fiercely guarded sanctuary. I want to control it all: the quiet, the comings and goings of familia and friends, the order of my day and night with Rafaelito.

I feel the waters of suppressed emotion rising under the

bridge between us, a lot of plain not-saying. I fear we may have taken this relationship, as partners and lovers, to its full course. I don't trust my fears, but cannot rid myself of this sense of hope- lessness. Are we slowly splitting off from each other?

Kids separate you. Kids bring you together. They literally separate you in the bed, worming their animal-selves between two grown women's breasts and hips and entangled thighs. They sneak into the bed at three o'clock in the morning, when they know you are too tired to resist. And our middle-aged mothers' bodies contort to make room for them, waking hours later with stiff necks and out-of-joint hips. Another night without sex. Nights become weeks. Weeks become months. Until someone finally wrestles the other into the bed, for the sheer lesbian pride of it, neither one of us willing to live a sexless life.

I remember that lesbian pride as we walked the streets of Provincetown with Rafaelito and Ellen's mother, many months ago, Nana's pale, freckled hand tucked into the crook of Ellen's arm. Ellen, ever observant, tells me, on the sly, how "different" the dynamic is when I am pushing Rafaelito in the stroller and she is guiding her mother down the crowded main drag.

"Now, that's interesting," she asserts. "The butch mom and her kid, the femme strolling with her mother. That's a compelling couple." When we change positions, Ellen is struck by the sudden absence of lingering covetous glances from the other dykes along the crowded main drag. "You walking with my mom, me pushing the stroller. The butch daughter, the femme mom with her child. Nah, that's predictable."

I love her for this. Her continued delight at our lesbianism, still savoring the "style" we generate from each other after so many years together. It is not superficial. It is hard won through great opposition. It is renewal, that mutual commitment to the rebellion of female loving, even into our forties. Ours is not domesticated loving. Keep your marriages, I say to myself. I want the freedom of this unpredictable desire. I want to stay awake.

Ellen comes in for a kiss and I turn my mouth to her cheek instead. She feels spurned. I explain it as my fear of giving her a cold. We know this is an excuse. We know this is not what I fear. We fight.

We fight in the morning. Then again in the evening. We fight because there is not enough room to want each other—not amid travel schedules and work weeks and child care and groceries and pediatricians and writing and not-writing and laundry and dishes and grant deadlines and meetings and more meetings. We fight about work: housework, artwork, political work. We fight about what is and is not our work.

"Practice what you preach," Ellen blazes me with her fiery tongue. Yet I remain removed. I do not wholly take risks in my public life. I am afraid of selling my soul to the devil. The devil of commerce, the devil of a feigned "commitment to community."

"Ambition is the enemy of art," I want to tell her. I don't tell her that I want to write like vocation, like spirit-saints calling me from the foot of the bed. This is the only religion I want to enter, the cloister of my own writer's cell. I am afraid of compromising the privacy I've learned to defend so passionately against all odds, against all causes. To write.

We fight, Rafael our silent witness.

He sits in his highchair in front of a bowl of bananas. He watches our faces. He doesn't yet fully understand all the words, but tone

and gesture tell him we are angry. Today I do not have enough time
to be both mom and playwright. Then suddenly, mid-argument,
Rafael points his finger at each of us and says, "No!"

We stop fighting. Kids bring you together.

La Causa

The other night, Ellen lamented the loss of socialism, the failure of
a realized victory for "even one country, the small size of El Sal-
vador." El Salvador, her emblem of resistance. She is remember-
ing that revolution, the romance of her engagement with it and
with her once-amor revolucionario.

I cry with her, but I am not she. I do not see myself in Tina
Modotti, who threw away her camera for communism. I will not
throw my "camera" away for any cause.

Still, Ellen's cause as a cultural organizer compels me. And
there are full days when I think only of giving her all the tacti-
cal support she needs to achieve it, to never abandon her. Ellen
asked me to find my own heart. She says she cannot stay with me
any longer if I do not examine my real feelings and be willing to
change. I am not open to Ellen. I don't know what to say to her.
I don't know how to come back. I am always protecting myself
from her. What do I fear she will take from me?

I remember one of the first times meeting Ellen, she walking
up the hill to greet me. I remember her smiling in a field of light.
This was the first sense I had of her, a brightness that enlivens, her
open heart. I am awed at times by that sudden beauty between
us—what is conjured spontaneously, sin trabajo. But it has felt so
long since those meetings of spirits. We are best just hanging out,
driving in the car, taking a little trip with Rafa. We are family

then. We are best just the three of us, no outside world pressing down upon us. Is it that world that divides?

Sueño

It is a Sonoran landscape. Cathy stands by my side. There are two paths in the dream. One high, one low, leading to the same destination. The lower path runs along the shoreline. We choose this one, follow it. The vista is breathtaking. A turquoise water lapping against a bleached Mexican desert sand. There are deer in the distance. They, too, are turquoise, the Native color of precious stone. We continue walking together.

Point Reyes, California

The sun has dropped to the level where the sand dunes seem to rise to catch it and the shadows of shore-lined bodies loom large and perfectly delineated in the wet-ribbed sand. Rafa is caught by the movement of the shadowing shapes. Still, I don't know if he quite understands the relationship between the motion of my now wildly waving hands and the dancing forms silhouetted in the sand. What he does discover, which thoroughly entertains him, are our "footprints" pressed into the sand, with each receding wave. It is the first time I've used the word with him, I realize, although not the first footprints we've made together. But these footprints are undeniable.

At first, he studies the deep outline shaped by my step, then jumps into it, his small step disappearing into my own. Only when I catch on that this is what fascinates him do I give it name and more shape in his child's imagination. He continues on down the beach, jumping with both feet now, shouting "footprints, footprints." I see his wonder, and then the sudden pause of dis-

appointment when he finds sand that doesn't adhere so readily. "Too wet," I tell him in one instance; "too hard, mijo," in another. In this way, we continue down the shore, greeting the delicate stream of each receding wave.

Then the words come to me. "Fall asleep to wake up"—that sudden forgetting of self in the act of wholly living a moment. It is a Zen notion to be sure, but seldom so completely realized except through the gift of one's teacher-son. Seeing through his fresh and innocent vision, Rafaelito is my lens, the prescription for these aging and forgetful eyes. All is about an acute awareness, waking up to those moments in our lives when there exists nothing else but this simple word, "footprint." My child's original mark upon the planet. "I am here, sweet earth," it proclaims. There is no yesterday, tomorrow, or last year. Yet there is all of it—the brittle bones of our antepasados, the heavy hearts of lovers, and whole years lost to sleep—which dissipates in the unselfconscious and thoroughly present naming of the imprint of a child's foot in the sand.

4

Blood Matters

1996

Día de Muertos

When my baby was born, he gave birth to a history.
His life, a road taken en compañía de los antepasados.

This, the binding thread of birth/death/rebirth
that we mexicanos forever bemoan
and ever celebrate

dancing drunk con el gusto de la vida
around the lip
of a grave.

*I*n the third year of our life together, Ellen moves out of our
home. *Not out of my arms or Rafa's reach, but into a peace of
mind, a piece of home she can call her own.*

The growing presence of Rafael in our lives filled up that space that
had once been reserved for Ellen and me together and apart: ourselves

as lovers, ourselves as creators, our selves that once had the luxury of picking up the slack when somebody else was slacking.

It was not an easy move to make, nor to counter the voices inside our heads arguing that this would mean the end of our family together. Maybe this is the gift of middle-aged loving, a more compassionate understanding of our own needs, our own natural limits. Easier to change a living arrangement than a cellular one.

What the move apart did do was lay bare all that sustained and separated Ellen and me beyond the domestic. Living together, our quarrels were not profound, and only on occasion profane. The deeper questions remained and lie buried beneath the stones of desire one carries inside their heart. The commitment we continued to make to each other was to slowly unearth those stones, one by one, as best we could. It was a "till life do we part" promise, and life sometimes does part us.

November 1996 / San Francisco

I stand in the kitchen with my sister. I dip my hands into the dishwater. I scrub, rinse, stack. She cries about the death of . . . what? Twenty years of a loveless marriage? More? Who can count when we stopped counting, stopped caring, only to stop mid-step, mid-life, and calculate with a vengeance how many good years left, good looks left, good waistlines, jawlines, bustlines? Men and time suddenly shrinking commodities in my sister's newly single mind, while four hundred miles south of here my uncle at seventy-six assumes the ninety-six-year-old dying body of my grandmother, his mother. How long ago was that death? I have to count to know.

I say to Jo Ann, "Life is about loss." She suffers over this, emerging enflamed from the fire of first real love at forty-five. We taste that life fleetingly, slipping through the sieve of our covetous hands.

Southern California

My Tío Bobby's hands are elegant in their sudden skeleton-shaped delicacy. His skin, a smooth glove of dried parchment. I could write the story of our lives there, in the steady caress of his hand, his softening face, so female. His female tears, his fears. He tells me, "I need the strength to face this. I am afraid I don't have the strength."

He is pure grace, my tío, always a class act, even in rumpled flannels. Even at death's door. Since the news of his impending death, I have been seeing that door in my day- and night-dreams like a silent movie running behind my eyeballs. I am reminded of how simple and child-like are the images we conjure of death: an ordinary wooden door opening to a black starless sky; a spaceman without his spacesuit, without the body inside the suit, floating.

We are all dumb animals. We know death is coming, the circle drawing tighter and tighter around us until we are pressed into the core-heart of the moment of that knowledge. And yet we continue to lie to ourselves that we are not my dying uncle, my mother in perhaps a decade of years, my baby's almost-lost life. Why do we think it won't happen to us? The length of our lives is a kind of cruel joke whether you're eight or eighty, watching the silver brilliance of death's blade enter. It splits open the sternum of our denial into two perfectly asymmetrical halves, the heart half-falling out of its home, still pulsing and animal alive. *I am not ready to stop. Not yet,* it laments.

We each find out we are to die within a fragment of a second in the cosmic hour. Still the giants give us time to prepare to fly, the body ages dramatically. We become old men overnight. We are as close to divine as we can get.

I see God in my tío because he is that close to death, closer than any-one I have ever known by heart, except for my son. I take my son to visit my dying uncle, to offer my uncle comfort and cariño, to bring my son closer to his history and his future. I will tell him years from now when it matters, "Yes, you met him. You knew him. You climbed upon the thin bones of his thighs and kissed him full-mouthed on the cheek. He cried. 'Angelito,' he always called you 'Angelito.'"

The next day my uncle is angry he cannot flick the ashes of the cigarette he is dying to have in the last days of lung cancer. He is too weak to make the long arm's journey from parched lip to doily-covered nightstand where the ashtray waits to receive him like a ghost. All the furniture talking now, telling stories about the lives they've seen pass through these doors.

She, the wife (the one not looking at God yet, only at her viejito dying) couldn't fall asleep unless she had his arm for a pillow under her head. She can't sleep now, holding her breath, waiting for God to take away her armrest. Tío's angry and Tía's sleepless and there's no rest for the wicked, we all fear. But there is no wickedness here. Only two human hearts dissolving.

I am trying to write about the impossible, the ordinary begin-ning of one life and the passing of another. Watching a life enter and another exit within the same brief moment of my family's history.

I dream my mother, Rafaelito, and I are standing on an outdoor elevated porch when an earthquake hits. I instantly grab my mother with one hand, my son with the other. At first, I enjoy the temblor's intensity and assure them both, "Just hold on. It'll pass." We ride the wave of the quake with tentative pleasure until suddenly it unexpectedly intensifies. The porch begins to

*collapse beneath us, the house next door caves in. I feel I am
losing hold of them both. As the quake rocks and rolls us I soon
realize we may not survive, and I try with all the strength in my
being to bring my son into me, to protect him from death. He is
slipping beyond my reach. My mother has left my consciousness.
I awaken.*

*Primordial struggle. Trying to hold onto she who precedes
me, he who follows. Forces beyond my control.*

My uncle is dying. Is this the first time in my life that pain has left me
empty of feeling? No broken heart/no welling tear ducts/no bruise or
blood? I had always named this hollow feeling "woman-hungry." But I
am not hungry. I am not lonely. I am empty, but not free.

Is it a crime to remember death in every waking moment of
one's life? Is it unnatural, unearthly? My son's dance—stockinged
feet kicking up the bedroom carpet, three-year-old, karate-chopping
hands flying—becomes a death dance because I think of nothing else
but to love and lose, to lose whom you love, to lose that you love.

*My parents have visited my dying uncle for what they know will
be the last time. They walk out of the small ground-floor apartment into the thin chill of a Southern Californian December.
They cross the lawn to their car, where my father unlocks and
holds open the door for my mother. She gets in. He goes around
to the driver's side and gets in. They sit side by side in their sweat-
ers in the front seat of the Buick and cry. Nobody ashamed of the
tears, nobody faking it. Together, they have known my uncle at
least as long as they have known each other, fifty years next year.
They cry together. Like old lovers.*

With the death of my querido tío I find myself having to explain my sudden absence of spirit, my mourning over a "mere" uncle. "He was like a father to me," I say, perfunctorily, hating the lie in the expression. My tío was not my father. I have a father. He was my uncle, my mother's younger brother whom she raised like a son in a family that does not separate cousin from sister from brother from blood. He was my uncle who fathered my younger cousin Cynthia, whose loss I suffer like a sister. He was my uncle. It matters.

My tío's death has ruptured that intimate circle of familia that is the last real generation of the Mexican American Moraga clan: those World War II veterans and their worker-wives having kids in the '40s and '50s, kids they hoped would be more than the bartenders, electronics assemblers, upholsterers, truck drivers, waitresses, housewives, railroad and factory workers they were. Some of us are more (economically and educationally), some of us aren't; but none of us are as much familia as they. And as my uncle's generation goes, la familia goes with it in that profoundly Mexican sense.

September 1995
Remembering—el lado paternal

We waited too long.

When we arrive, Rafaelito's paternal grandfather is already in a coma. We waited because Ricardo, so new to queer fatherhood, didn't know if it was his place to ask. I didn't know if it was our place to go. Both Ricardo and I trying to figure out what blood and bones had to do with this business of making queer familia. But we're Mexicans. Blood matters. So, at the last minute, I take Rafaelito to Los Angeles to visit his "tata," Ricardo's dying father—comunista, doctor, y revolucionario in his own right.

*Rafaelito is not allowed to enter any further than the door of
the ICU room. His tender age makes him too vulnerable to the
deadly infection Tata carries in his lungs. I take hold of Tata's
sleeping hand and sense in it a living electric current that passes
between this dying man and his grandson whom Ricardo holds
in his arms. It is a mutual connection. There is no explaining this;
my son and his tata have never met.*

A full year after his father's death, Ricardo tells me, "I know
my father is gone. I don't feel his presence, but he speaks to the
kids." He means his nieces, especially Fiona, the youngest, who casu-
ally refers to her tata as if he still occupied a place at the dinner table,
on the couch, in the sun on the front porch steps.

"He speaks to Rafael, too," I tell Ricardo.

*And as my altar clutters with the images of those who have
passed on, my child learns the sacredness of candlelight and
murmured prayer. Do I hear their voices, the voices of the dead?
I don't know. At times, I pray quietly, with no resonance other
than the vibration of my own silent wording within the tempo-
ral geography of my body. But Rafael is listening, watching. I
hear him respond to my calling of his tata's and tío's names,
announcing, "Amen."*

Día de Lupe
*My uncle died on the feast day of the Immaculate Conception on
December 8, 1996. Four days later, on December 12, he is buried*

on el Día de la Virgen de Guadalupe. And in the span of those two feast days—the first to honor the European Virgin Mother, the second to honor the Indigenous—the story of my uncle and all my familia is told: US-born and Mexican.

At my uncle's funeral, my father, a man unaccustomed to speaking in public, mounts the pulpit and declares aloud to the congregation, "He was my brother." My father is a gringo. But Mexican is the only way we know how to make familia.

EPILOGUE

MESSENGER OF DEATH

1997

When you told me about the funeral, it amazed me how we/they acknowledge you as the family scribe, the "seer." How rare it is that a family can see and appreciate that across differences and generations. It is because your work, your life honors them.

—letter from Ellen

A Sunday Morning

Ellen and I converse and caress in bed, arms and legs draped around each other. She and I have grown closer since her move, the desire returning. I feel her softening and I, too, soften to the touch. She has lost a lot of weight (from nerves and overwork mostly), but her body has a suppleness to it, a vulnerability that invites me. There are times I feel her skin moving slowly into aging (that quality of softening). At other times, the softness feels like a kind of rejuvenation and a laying down of arms.

I admit I miss the "daily" with Ellen at times, as does Rafa, I know. Still, for us, less has proved best. "I can't try and follow the rules no more," I had told Ellen. "No more 'this is what a couple is supposed to look like.' We are what a couple looks like! We are what a family looks like."

Suddenly, the drumroll of two small bare feet can be heard from the next bedroom. They speed across the living room hardwood floor and then across the kitchen into our bedroom where they lift off the ground, transporting their pajama-clad, Pooh Bear–towing owner onto our bed. Rafa muscles his way in between Ellen and me, throwing his arms around my neck. "My mami," he asserts. Playing along, Ellen retorts, "My girlfriend." Rafa ups the ante, "My girlfriend." And the "custody battle" over mamá ensues. Ellen's and my eyes meet. We don't speak to it, but the joy we draw from this love triangle is sublime.

I watch Rafael, at three years old, take on the characteristics of Ellen's animated humor, her flare for the dramatic and simple righteousness. There is no accounting for love. No accounting for what finally makes a family, except love. I remain awed by this mystery of how love and blood and home and history and desire coalesce and collide to construct a child's sense of self and family. I know blood quantum does not determine parenthood any more than it determines culture. Still, I know blood matters. It just does not matter more than love.

An hour later, Rafael and Ellen have fallen back asleep. I rise, Ellen stirs in bed. Her presence is well-placed and rides deep in me, lingering as I slip out of the covers and into sweatpants, and slipper my way into my study.

From its window, I write with the view of the overgrown clover-filled garden: the giant cedar split vertically at its peak after a harsh winter's storm, the bald spot of exposed fence where once a tree sprawled, diseased and beautiful. It was uprooted and carried away in a dumpster. To my left, the skeletal frame of a fruit tree, never bearing fruit. To my right, the umbrella of an avocado tree, also childless.

I suspect my description of all this, including the fallen telephone line tangled in the barbed wire of the driveway gate, calls forth little beauty in the imagination. But all is lovely to me and changing. It has just begun to rain, ever so delicately, so lightly it can't be heard. I can only see it silver against the deep forest-green backdrop of the cedar. Rafa's toys abandoned in the winter cold are now being engulfed by the growing clover. They are bright spots of primary plastic colors amid the complexity of nature's hues.

I love this place. This spot of chaos and growth amid industrial San Francisco. My home. Maybe I write this way because I sense I am leaving this place of rose-colored geraniums and blossoming lavender sage. Are those irises breaking through the mound of clover and succulents? It feels good to write like this, my woman and child sleeping. It feels good to write "my woman and child" without ambivalence.

The flame from my altar candle dances in a double (vaguely triple) mirror reflection in the window. It is raining harder now and the flame insists: *change*.

The hardest loving is what is required of me as a mother: the ever letting go as the feelings deepen between my son and me. How can I describe the lesson that with each day there is a birth and a dying of this time in our lives together; that with a child one sees it so clearly because the changes are physically and dramatically manifested?

Rafael Angel had been my messenger of death, not in any negative sense of the word, but in the profound comprehension of the unsparing miracle of the cycle of our lives. I could write that he is a messenger of life, but I know it is truer to acknowledge that my sometimes-quiet sadness at the deepest moments of joy with my child has to do with this complete knowledge of impermanence.

In the face of that knowledge, I visit my aging parents, bring my woman coffee in bed, and stroke the silk of my son's hair.

This, too, will pass.

Afterword

100 Nights

Rafael Angel Moraga

The circumstances of my birth were always a topic of conversation during family gatherings, often described cinematically, like a movie logline: the emergency ride to Hollywood Kaiser; my two-pound, palm-size self; then the private helicopter from LA to San Francisco; the discovery of a deadly disease and the surgery that would ensue; the battle I won in a life-and-death struggle—me against my infected intestines.

It was the Harry Potter effect: the scar that marked me a survivor and cast me in a familial epic.

I have often felt like an outlier in my mother's immediate biological family, born too early, but also nearly a decade too late to join that last round of first cousins. Still, I was proud to be a Moraga whose melanin matched my elders as shade was fading with each new generation.

As a kid, my medical "tattoos" were fodder for elementary school bullies and classmates. They would make faces of disgust, gesturing to my fungus-ravaged toes* and surgical scars. At the beach, I would hide

---

* Believed to be related to an overload of antibiotics as an infant.

my feet deep in the sand or under a towel at the pool, often resisting swimming altogether. I just couldn't rid myself of the weight of their criticism, and worst of all from those closest to me. I was constantly fielding questions and being asked to bare my surgical markings as a kind of curiosity.

Although most of that shame has subsided, the long-term physical side effects have not. I still constantly monitor my diet, performing gastronomic gymnastics to navigate food sensitivities and reactions that wreak havoc on my tormented surgically repaired intestines. As I grew older, the hyper-vigilance regarding my health gave rise to a prevailing hypochondria, in which every minor ache and pain felt as if it might be a death sentence. All this amplified during the COVID-19 pandemic. And yet the one thing that did not rock me were the lockdowns and the isolation. They were not new to me.

In 1993, I spent the first three formative months of my life alone, similarly "incubated." In an odd way, this imposed isolation became my comfort zone. Regardless of the exhaustive visits from my mother and loved ones, nurses were the consistent presence. I spent the first one hundred nights of my life without a secure sense of family connection, separated from the rest of the world.

Now, at twenty-eight years old, these are experiences that I have leaned on. Early in my life, I learned that I am in charge of defining my own existence. My grandmother, who had half her stomach removed during my mother's childhood, faced a choice to continue fighting or give up, and she chose the former. So did I.

I have lived my life with an awareness of an intrinsic vulnerability. I have long struggled to both define and free my consciousness in relation to the most traumatic event of my life: my birth. I have no cognitive memory of this. It is an emotional and physical recall that has seriously impacted who I have become in adulthood, and has been a constant issue in therapy sessions. What I do know is that whatever person I was going to be immediately changed the moment I went under the knife at three weeks old. I lost the shimmer that newborns are born with, that glow of life.

I will never know the Rafa I could have been, the Rafa who was taken from me. I can never get him back. And yet there is a part of me that will always value the experience. The same could be said for my mother, watching her newborn baby wheeled off for the fight of his new life, she too was transformed by this trauma. Of course, this is what *Wings* is about—the responsibility and weight of motherhood hit her with full force from the very beginning. Any preparation that she had all fell out the window when I was born three months premature.

The events surrounding my birth have made our connection stronger than any DNA. We have faced life's greatest adversities together, and not once did my mother ever treat me like damaged goods or a child to be Bubble-Wrapped through life. She let me scrape my knee, move about the city without protest or consternation, and most of all to use the same determination I had from birth to stand up for myself and others; to face discrimination and inequality even when there was no one by my side. I have been formed by a laborer's mentality, my mother's typing away at her computer from sunrise to sunset to bring forth the world she sees in her mind: from my grandmother's arthritic factory hands that held up a generation, to my grandfather's lunch-pail optimism that has led him to the precipice of a centenarian year.

Growing up in Oakland, California, my family was the Addams Family on the block. My mom, stepmother Celia, and my sister, Camerina (Celia's granddaughter), made up the only queer familia of color in a predominately white neighborhood. Even in Oakland during the early 2000s, the outside world did not reflect the people who sat at our kitchen table. My parents raised me in a community of Black and Brown artists, educators, entrepreneurs, and community organizers that became my bedrock. Most of them were also queer, but I didn't think about that because this international community was my family. They put the time in to get to know me during sleepy post-ceremony tamaladas and post-holiday Tres Reyes festivities. My house served as a place of refuge especially for queer women of color. For more than twenty years, Celia offered sweat lodges and other traditional ceremonies in our backyard for those who needed them, and my mother kept the fire.

Looking back, I see now all the mix of cultures and identities that passed through my childhood home were also the primary reason I have always had an eagerness for exploration. Since graduating high school a decade ago, I have learned and lived in Chicago, Los Angeles, Madrid, Rome, London, Minneapolis, and New York, never staying in one place for more than two years. Traveling alone, this nomadic life gave me a type of anonymity that I also needed; not the "writer's son," nor a Mexican Harry Potter, but simply a global citizen. I look at my scars now not as a hindrance, but as a reminder of what I am capable of.

These two long years of the pandemic have been my second incubation. They have given me the time to revisit much of what has defined me—the isolation and the fear. I know now that I will re-emerge on the other side of this plastic void with renewed ganas. My life was cultivated with the fortitude of Chicana familial consciousness, forged by our ancestors from the deserts of Sonora and the mountains of Durango. I am a man made of stitches and staples, but will no longer burrow my feet in the sand. I can spread my toes wide toward the ocean, knowing there is a future beyond the horizon. I just need to go and live it.

February 2022

Some Character Backstory

In 1989, I met **Ellen** (Gavin) through our shared work in theater; she, as the founder and artistic director of Brava! Women for the Arts in San Francisco and I, as a playwright. Under Ellen's leadership, Brava produced three world premieres of my plays (1990–1996).

Ricardo (Bracho) was a student in my Chicano Studies Creative Writing and Theater classes at UC Berkeley from the late 1980s to 1991. Over the years of our ensuing friendship and his emergence as a playwright and a queer Chicano cultural activist in San Francisco, we collaborated on multiple projects, including DramaDIVAS, a project of Brava! Women for the Arts (1991–1995).

Cathy (Arellano) is a Chicana poet, originally from the Mission District of San Francisco. I first met Cathy in fall 1987 when she was a student at UC Berkeley and I, a lecturer in Chicano Studies. In the course of a year, Cathy and I, along with writer Carla Trujillo, would form "La Familia," the first openly gay and lesbian Latino/a campus organization in California. Cathy has remained a constant in Rafael's and my life ever since.

Sources

Allison. Dorothy. *Two or Three Things I Know for Sure*. New York: Dutton, 1995.

Matthews. Tede. "Angel Wings" (unpublished poem).

Monette. Paul. *Borrowed Time*. New York: Harcourt Brace Jovanovich, 1988.

de Montaigne. Michel. *The Essays of Michel de Montaigne*, Translated and Edited by M. A. Screech. London: Allen Lane, 1991.

Morrison. Toni. *Jazz*. New York: Alfred P. Knopf, 1992.

Silko. Leslie Marmon. *Almanac of the Dead*. New York: Simon & Schuster, 1991.

Acknowledgments

First who come to mind in gratitude are Anthony Arnove and Rachel Cohen of Haymarket Books. Thank you, Anthony for responding to my illustrious agent's inquiry to re-issue my earlier works with such enthusiasm. At the mere mention of bringing *Wings* (a much beloved book to me personally) out of obscurity, you responded with a resounding "yes." Your support, along with Rachel's sound production skills and her generous patience made for a seamless collaborative experience. I thank Jim Plank, as publicist for this project, and Jesse Fleming, as copyeditor. All in all, it's a pleasure to work again with a leftist press; to be in your political company and that of your cadre of compelling authors.

I am beholden, beyond all measure, to Stuart Bernstein, my literary agent. He has a deep faith in me, which I continue to marvel at; how it somehow augments my ability to produce even at the hardest of times. As a writer, this is a gift from the gods. Thank you, Stuart, for the laughter. I owe you a few cocktails.

Of course, there are the "characters" of this work that I thank for courageously bearing witness to those years of struggle; they are my blood and heart relations here and gone.

Today, twenty-five years later, I am surrounded by queer familia, closer than I had ever imagined—my beloved Celia, my almost-hija Cath, and the families they both bring with them. *Es un milagro de amor* I think. And, then there's, Rafa . . . who has returned to us as son and brother and tío at once. Thanks for coming home.

For a moment, we are all just a bit more whole.

About Haymarket Books

Haymarket Books is a radical, independent, nonprofit book publisher based in Chicago. Our mission is to publish books that contribute to struggles for social and economic justice. We strive to make our books a vibrant and organic part of social movements and the education and development of a critical, engaged, and internationalist Left.

We take inspiration and courage from our namesakes, the Haymarket Martyrs, who gave their lives fighting for a better world. Their 1886 struggle for the eight-hour day—which gave us May Day, the international workers' holiday—reminds workers around the world that ordinary people can organize and struggle for their own liberation. These struggles—against oppression, exploitation, environmental devastation, and war—continue today across the globe.

Since our founding in 2001, Haymarket has published more than nine hundred titles. Radically independent, we seek to drive a wedge into the risk-averse world of corporate book publishing. Our authors include Angela Y. Davis, Arundhati Roy, Keeanga-Yamahtta Taylor, Eve Ewing, Aja Monet, Mariame Kaba, Naomi Klein, Rebecca Solnit, Olúfẹ́mi O. Táíwò, Mohammed El-Kurd, José Olivarez, Noam Chomsky, Winona LaDuke, Robyn Maynard, Leanne Betasamosake Simpson, Howard Zinn, Mike Davis, Marc Lamont Hill, Dave Zirin, Astra Taylor, and Amy Goodman, among many other leading writers of our time. We are also the trade publishers of the acclaimed Historical Materialism Book Series.

Haymarket also manages a vibrant community organizing and event space in Chicago, Haymarket House, the popular Haymarket Books Live event series and podcast, and the annual Socialism Conference.

Also Available
from Haymarket Books

All the Blood Involved in Love
Maya Marshall

Angela Davis: An Autobiography
Angela Y. Davis

Community as Rebellion: A Syllabus for Surviving Academia
as a Woman of Color
Lorgia García Peña

There Are Trans People Here
H. Melt

Black Queer Hoe
Britteney Black Rose Kapri, foreword by Danez Smith

My Mother Was a Freedom Fighter
Aja Monet

Undivided Rights: Women of Color Organizing for Reproductive Justice
Marlene Gerber Fried, Elena Gutiérrez, Loretta Ross, and Jael Silliman

How We Get Free: Black Feminism and the Combahee River Collective
Edited by Keeanga-Yamahtta Taylor

Mama Phife Represents: A Memoir
Cheryl Boyce-Taylor

About the Authors

Cherríe Moraga is an internationally recognized poet, essayist, and playwright whose professional life began in 1981 with her coeditorship of the groundbreaking feminist anthology *This Bridge Called My Back: Writings by Radical Women of Color*. The author of several collections of her own writings, including *A Xicana Codex of Changing Consciousness, Loving in the War Years,* and *Waiting in the Wings: Portrait of a Queer Motherhood*, Moraga is the recipient of the United States Artists Rockefeller Fellowship for Literature and the American Studies Association Lifetime Achievement Award, among numerous other honors. As a dramatist, her awards include an NEA, two Fund for New American Plays Awards, and the PEN/West Award. In the fall of 2017, she began her tenure as a professor in the department of English at the University of California, Santa Barbara, where with her artistic partner, Celia Herrera Rodríguez, she founded Las Maestras

Center: Xicana[x] Indigenous Thought, Art, and Social Praxis. Her most recent work, *Native Country of the Heart*, a memoir, was published by Farrar, Straus and Giroux.

Rafael Angel Moraga is an actor and writer from Oakland, California. He graduated from UCLA in 2017 with a degree in World Arts & Cultures and received his master's in writing for stage & broadcast media from the Royal Central School of Speech and Drama in 2018. Prior to the COVID pandemic, he worked as an actor with BIPOC theatre organizations such as New Native Theatre in Minneapolis, Minnesota. He is currently based in Sacramento, California.